My Early Years in Europe, Africa and Asia

George Lowell Tollefson

PALO FLECHADO PRESS

Copyright © 2024 George Lowell Tollefson

All rights reserved.

ISBN: 978-1-952026-11-9

Library of Congress Control Number: 2024922054

Cover Design by White Rabbit Arts at The Historical Fiction Company

Palo Flechado Press, Santa Fe, New Mexico

OTHER WORK BY GEORGE LOWELL TOLLEFSON

Philosophical Works
The Immaterial Structure of Human Experience
The Limits of Reason
The Thinking Process

Key to the Philosophy of Immaterialism
The System of the Mind
Thoughts on Creativity, Spirit, and the Ethical Life
Unbridled Democracy

Extracts from **Unbridled Democracy**
Ethical Considerations
Moral Democracy
Spirit as Universal Consciousness
The Thinking Arts

Essays
A Healer of Nations
Capitalism and Democracy
In The Hearts of the People (out of print)
What Is War?

Fiction
Barnyard Fable
Bigger Than The Facts
Conversations: Jesus and His Disciples
From The Deer Forest
God Save The Queen

Lonely People
Season of Mists
The Golden Grain (out of print)

Poetry and Aphorisms
Vietnam War Elegy
Song of the Spirit
Solitudes of Thought (out of print)

Table of Contents

Prefatory Note

Washington, DC, and Virginia 1

Paris, France, and South Bend, Indiana 4

Virginia 8

Morocco 13

Germany 18

Tokyo, Japan 28

The Philippines: Preadolescence 31

The Philippines: The Early Teens 68

Northern Japan 81

Southern Japan 97

Stateside 110

Marine Training: Boot Camp 114

Marine Training: Infantry Training Regiment 119

Supply School and Barstow 125

Language School 128

Vietnam: Division and Regiment 132

Vietnam: The Battalion 139

Vietnam: Phu Bai 179

Stateside 195

For Loretta Marie, my wife and friend,
who has also painstakingly proofread this manuscript

Prefatory Note

This is a memoir primarily of my early years, most of which were spent overseas in France, Morocco, Germany, the Philippines, Japan, and Vietnam. It is not a work of art. So there is nothing contrived or added. It is truthfully related insofar as my memory can muster long forgotten facts over a period of so many years. After coming home from the Vietnam War at the age of twenty-two, I have never again lived abroad.

My reason for writing this memoir has been to provide a slightly different perspective – mine, of course – on an important historical period. None of this outlook is to be valued in its own right, particularly since I was a child during most of these years. But it is a private view which may have some interest in spite of this, since we are all human beings caught in events which we are often compelled to navigate without a full understanding of their nature. Such simple beings as we are do make up the greater part of the substance of history.

Again, I wish to emphasize that I have written the truth here without exaggeration or modification. I have done so to the best of my ability, insofar as a distant memory will serve me. I waited as long as I did to write this in the hope that I might be past the age of vanities, if that is possible.

George Lowell Tollefson

My Early Years
in
Europe, Africa and Asia

George Lowell Tollefson

Washington, DC, and Virginia

The year is 2024. I am an old man now, seventy-eight a few months ago, and I am doing what people do in their final years. I am looking back and asking myself: Have I lived a productive life? Did I do the things I set out to do? And did I do them well? Not an easy thing to determine. By the standards of the world, I have not. For I chose to be a writer, and little recognition has followed upon my efforts. But did I write well? I believe the answer is yes, for the most part. No writer is consistently a master of his or her craft. But in general my work has been what I sought to make it. And that is the most anyone can do.

So now I turn my telescope homeward. That is to say, I look far back to the beginning and try to remember what I can, ever with an eye to understanding what formed me and what I did. To begin with, of course, I was born in 1946. It happens. I do not remember it. But I have been told it is the case, and being born seems to have been the case with everyone I know. So I will take my mother's word for it.

She was generally pretty honest with me, quite straightforward in fact. Though there were quibbles here and there, as there are with the generality of humankind. We all have things we would rather modify to improve our self image, or to raise a child on a straighter path than we perceive ourselves to have followed. In this case, she was not always completely honest about her boyfriends, when she had them.

George Lowell Tollefson

You see, she was separated from my father before I was born and divorced shortly thereafter. A particular quibble I have in mind occurred when I was about fourteen. We were living in the Philippines, and her boyfriend was the chief of police for the town of Angeles, just outside Clark Air Force Base. He would come to visit, and they would go into her bedroom for awhile. She told me they were just napping. I was fourteen, for God's sake. This is the modern world. What does a fourteen-year-old not know, at least in hearsay or theory? Nevertheless, I did not question her judgement. It was none of my business.

As to my birth, mine was a seven month premature arrival. I probably did some yelling. But I do not remember. I have always been temperamental. "Mental temper" my mother always called it. Pretty insightful. It is a bit of anger without any firepower behind it. It fizzles as soon as it flashes out of its human gun barrel. This can be embarrassing in a public setting.

According to my mother, I was kept in an incubator for awhile. I was circumcised: a bit of a botched jab leaving a scar. But I survived intact. Then, according to her, I was sent home "to die." I did know her to exaggerate on occasion. But there may have been truth in it. She said I was burned in the incubator. My first sun tan. I am a bit pale skinned, even for a whitey. Pale skinned, long boned, and thin as a rake I was as a child. But small boned as well. In fact, my mother had the smallest hands I have ever seen. Yet she was five nine and a half in height. I took after her. I grew to be five eleven.

These events took place in Washington, DC, except for my growing to be five eleven. Because my mother had a full time

My Early Years in Europe, Africa and Asia

job, I was farmed out to some people in Franconia, Virginia, by the name of Walker. I boarded with them. My mother came to see me on weekends. The Walkers lived on a defunct farm in a big old farmhouse. It was wonderful. Some of their sons were building new houses on the property, so I had playmates, some good, some not so good. I lived there until I was two and a half, then again between the ages of five and seven.

George Lowell Tollefson

Paris, France, and South Bend, Indiana

My mother worked for the State Department. She was Averell Harriman's administrative assistant, i.e., secretary. In 1948 she went to Paris as a more distant member of his staff. I went with her. I was a slow talker, so I did not learn to do so until I was in Paris, spending most of my time with an Italian governess named Beatrice. She spoke French (or possibly Italian) to me, so that was the language I spoke. Consequently, my mother needed her to translate for me.

I remember in particular a nightmare in which my teddy bear was coming down at me from the ceiling. I started yelling and crying in terror. I can still see that bear coming down at me in the dark. I have never been fond of bears since. I think the whole thing resulted from Beatrice telling me the European version of "Goldilocks and the Three Bears," which does not end pleasantly.

At any rate, I was brought out of my room and set upon a little table. There I related my adventure, and Beatrice repeated everything I said to my mother. I could not understand what the problem was. Why did everything have to be repeated? I think in images, so I now remember the episode as though it had taken place in English, though I was not speaking it at the time.

I also remember noisy trucks unloading in the dark, as Beatrice and I went out very early for the day's groceries. We lived on a street that radiated off from what had been the site of the Bastille. On the way home, we always stopped off at a bakery and bought a fresh loaf of French bread. It would still be warm, and she would break off an end and give it to me. Heaven. The aroma! The taste!

The only other thing I clearly remember is the public urinals. The wall of the facility did not come to the ground, and you could see the men's feet lined up at the common trough. She would send me into one of those, where she could keep track of my doings by watching the progress of my feet among the many larger ones.

She took me home with her to northern Italy at some point. My mother let her do this. That is how much she trusted her. I do not remember the trip, of course. At least, I do not think I do. Very early memories like these float around in a kind of indistinct soup in the depths of the mind. It took me years just to resurrect the ones about France. For many years I thought they were memories of Morocco, which came later.

During the year in Paris, my mother met a man she later came to despise. But at this point, having been divorced from my father, she was ready for a new husband and home. A nice home was something she craved all her life and never got. She had grown up in a comfortable home in Hastings, Nebraska, and that upbringing was always her life standard.

At the age of three, she had been adopted and was raised by her paternal grandparents. That made her three uncles her brothers, along with her natural brother. Her father had died, and her mother was too poor to raise the two of them. She (her mother) had another older son by a prior husband, whom she also outlived, not to mention the third and last one which she outlived as well. So she kept the older son and raised him.

My mother's adopted father (called Papa, since he was her grandfather) was a college professor, who had once been a pharmacist. He had originally had money, much of which was lost in the Depression. So she grew up with all the niceties of etiquette and furnishings. She always looked forward to the same, and that is what this guy, an American in Paris, promised her.

He was going to give her a big home, since he supposedly was well placed in the Studebaker Corporation. Not true. All a lie. But we did not know it until we returned to the States and moved to South Bend, Indiana. He was somewhere low in the guts of the corporate machine. We lived in a dark, grubby little house in a grubby part of town, as I remember.

I have three principal memories of that time. One was knocking over my glass of milk with my elbow whenever I got the opportunity. Another was having to eat some awful canned tomato soup on a regular basis. It must have been cheap. And the last was my new stepfather dragging my mother across the bed by the hair. She had apparently informed him she was going to leave him.

After performing the above feat, he asked me at age four who I would rather be with. I chose Mom. No further memories here. My mind does that. Blocks out all sorts of things, if they are inconvenient. Blocked out nightmares of the Vietnam War for twelve years. There may be other things from the archaic past I have yet to recognize. Probably never will.

Well, we got out of that one, and my mother never trusted men after that. It was really her third disappointment. Before

My Early Years in Europe, Africa and Asia

she met my father she had been in love with a Cherokee Indian from Oklahoma, who was in the Marine Corps. This was during the second world war, and he shipped out to the Pacific theater. He wrote her regularly, but her landlady did not approve of the racial mix. So she withheld the letters. This went on for at least a year before my mother discovered the problem. She thought he had not written. He eventually came home and married his high school girlfriend.

My mother always insisted I would have been the same person if she had married him. Temperament and all. Poor guy. I am sure he would not have passed on such a thing as my temperament. Frankly, I have always thought that if I had a chance at a second life in this world I would not take it. Beautiful but nasty place.

Mostly people make it so, myself included, no doubt. Funny though. I do want to live this life for as long as I can. There is no explaining the oddities of human nature. Maybe it is because I have a nice wife and nice, now grown kids, not to mention grandchildren. The latter take on special meaning when you get old.

George Lowell Tollefson

Virginia

What followed our various adventures with Mr. Falsehood was my return to the Walkers in Virginia after my mother had completed divorce proceedings in Pasadena, California, prior to this and her going to work for the Defense Department as a court reporter and being sent to what was then French Morocco. The Moroccans did not care much for the French part of the above nomenclature for their country and periodically knifed French citizens in the street and set their cars afire.

But Americans were not disliked at this point, and my mother loved that part of the world better than any other. She had numerous adventures, such as dressing as a man to go on an investigation in one of the medinas, where women were apparently not supposed to be. Some Moroccan slipped by in the crowded market thoroughfare and yanked off her hat, revealing her long hair.

She worked for the Air Force legal office at Sidi Slimane Air Base near Rabat. There was a guard at her apartment building who became a close friend. Later, when I was there, we went to what my mother said was some kind of wedding reception at his house. We must have arrived after the ceremony, considerably afterwards. All we did was drink tea with his family at his house. No one else was present. The house was one of those concrete affairs that fall in on people during earthquakes.

My Early Years in Europe, Africa and Asia

Before I joined my mother in Morocco, I spent two more years at the Walkers, from the age of five to the age of seven. I have warm memories of the time. It was a beautiful property for a child. At one point I remember discovering a guinea hen nest with some other kids, grandchildren of the Walkers. There were dozens of eggs in the nest, a sort of communal deposit. We gathered up a bunch of them and were breaking them open on the sidewalk to see if they would fry. It was a very hot day. But somehow I disturbed a yellow jacket nest, and my reaction to the stings brought Mrs. Walker to the rescue. She was not pleased with the broken egg display on the walkway, so she made us gather up the remaining eggs in a bucket. These supplied us with breakfast for some time. Rather gamey, as I recall.

There were other pleasantries. Mrs. Walker made bread on Saturday. I guess it took awhile to rise, so we would have the worst meal of the week that night: hot dogs, sauerkraut, and little white powdered donuts. Awful. I mean the sauerkraut and pretty much the donuts as well. There are better donuts in the world.

But, ah, the next morning. That is when the glory of the celestial realm would burst over the countryside, especially on a sunny day, and there were many of those in Virginia. On Sunday morning Mrs. Walker would make puffs, a good many of them. They were similar to New Mexico's sopapillas: triangles of fried bread. But they were much larger. After breakfast, I would run outdoors into the sunshine with my pockets full of them.

George Lowell Tollefson

As compensation for my joy – life always has its compensations – I would be too full to eat the big family afternoon dinner. Mashed potatoes, roast beef, green beans, dressings, various salads, everything you can think of, all of it piled heavily onto my plate for my own good. I was a bit of a rail of a kid. And in America that is not considered healthy. You are supposed to roll like a beach ball. Quite a few members of the Walker family would be present at the big meal, but I would still be sitting there long after they had all adjourned from the table. Sitting there in the dark, trying to figure out how to finish this unwanted feast.

I took my naps on the front porch in the cool summer breeze – enforced naps.

The Walkers had a string of chickens at one point. Half a dozen, all white, more or less. Apparently, they were Easter chicks bought in eggs injected with colored dye. There were still traces of the color in their feathers when I first encountered them. It must have been shortly after I arrived at the age of five. They were a striking wonder to me with their nervous, lively movements and habits. I was hooked.

Later I had chickens in the Philippines. I always found them fascinating. The Walker chickens I first encountered coming around from the back of the separate garage in single file, clucking and pecking the ground. They were about half grown. But, alas, the Walkers had a big white brown-spotted bird dog, probably a pointer. He finished them all off.

At this time the Walker place was surrounded by other large properties, predominantly vacant in the sense of this being country living. It was paradise. I have always wanted to duplicate it. But maybe that is just an excuse for wanting to go back to one's childhood. In later life there is a perceived lack of complications in memories of early childhood. But of course that is a lie. Life is never easy.

When I was an infant, I probably fussed over the fact that I thought the contents of my milk bottle were tainted. If I did, that would have been sometime between my first and second stay at the Walkers. I was about three. They had a goat there for me when we visited because I could not drink cow's milk. So I must have visited for awhile, with and without my mother's presence.

I was locked up at one point during that visit in a chained-link fenced area. I do not know why. The space was full of old tires, tin cans, myself, and the goat. I expected the goat to eat the cans and was disappointed not to observe this. The science of life is always changing as one gets older. Or is this the philosophy of life? I was a budding philosopher, but did not know it. I had a lot to learn involving large quantities of turned-over expectations.

Sometime during my second long stay, toward the end of my time there when I was seven, I was talked by some of my friends into doing a little thievery. I was being sent to the store – a bit of a country walk – to pick up a loaf of bread and some other items. In the process, I lifted a candy bar. I thought I had done a good job of it, but when I got home I found that the store owner had called to let Mrs. Walker know I was carrying contraband. I was duly apprehended, given a small verbal lesson in the virtue of honesty, and sent back to the store, not only to return the candy bar but to apologize.

George Lowell Tollefson

I also got my mouth washed out with soap at one point for exercising it around a few choice words. That was earlier. Strange, even a child's profanity, like "kaka," is made up of four letter words. They do roll off the tongue nicely, even as an adult. But nobody is washing mouths out these days.

At age seven I finally got word that I was leaving to join my mother in North Africa. All my local friends heard was "Africa," so they regaled me with tales of rogue lions, leopards, and pythons crawling through windows. A woman friend of my mother had to return to the US for a short time, so she was tasked with bringing me back with her to Morocco, which she did. We paddled all the way in a canoe. Well, not quite. Our rations would not have held out.

My Early Years in Europe, Africa and Asia

Morocco

Once there, I began life in an apartment building in Port Lyautey, Morocco. Among other things, the apartment had a balcony and something that resembled a bidet. The bidet was not on the balcony, of course. It was in a corner of the living room. Good for sudden access, I suppose. I was told it was for washing one's feet. Handy. As for the balcony, what I remember is the sparrows. I was convinced I could communicate with them. So I would lie on the floor just inside the room and cheep away. It did not result in any personal relationships.

There was a pond in a park down the street, so one day I snuck out of the apartment while my mother was at work and fished for tadpoles in the pond. Nobody bothered me, but I was counseled not to do that anymore.

Our time in town did not last. My mother seemed to have a penchant for living out in the middle of nowhere, far from the prying eyes of her American associates. She was in many ways a private person, as I turned out to be, perhaps in emulation of her. But there were other ways in which she was not so private, and I usually found those embarrassing.

I remember being at a diner counter somewhere – I believe Chicago, where she was visiting her natural mother. She was dipping cubes of sugar in her coffee and giving them to me while she talked to my grandmother. Something in her manner made me feel a little too conspicuous and foolish standing there beside her. But I cannot remember precisely what it was.

At any rate, she was always very confident with people to the point of believing some of them liked her when they did not. I have always been oversensitive to that sort of thing, and I have never been particularly confident with people, unless I knew them well. I do not trust the average Joe, I suppose. Never have.

But I have always tried to treat everyone as if I had the highest respect for them. Maybe they see through it because I have occasionally gotten a response implying weakness on my part. I generally toughen up after that, but it is a little late and requires some persuading. It is usually the less educated, less intelligent types who arrive at such conclusions. Cannot see past surface appearances, I suppose.

As for our move from the apartment in Morocco, we headed for the countryside to somewhere within commuting distance of Sidi Slimane Air Base, but not too close. We always had to live off base, "on the economy" as the phrase went. Official policy for nonmilitary personnel. That was okay with me, not that I had any opinion to express, or leave to do so. Seven-year-olds were to "be seen and not heard." As often as not, I would just as soon not be seen either. And where we settled on this occasion fit the bill. It was on a farm with citrus (lime and lemon) orchards stretching out behind the house.

We had a live-in housekeeper, which, I came to learn then, we always would have for the next ten years overseas. The US dollar was very strong after the second world war, allowing for such things. Usually the housekeeper was our cook too. But I cannot remember if Fatima was. That was her name.

More interesting from my point of view, she had a cat named Peuch, pronounced peeooch, as in "Oh, does that smell" with a ch on the end. If I remember right, the cat's fur was some sort of mixture of white and tan, perfect for Moroccan desert life. Not that Morocco is all desert. But a good part of it is hot, arid, and sandy.

Peuch arrived in a wicker basket. Once released from the basket, it took off and lived happily ever after in the orchards. Fatima was never able to win it back. Life was just too good out there. The place was loaded with rats close to half its own size. It would have been like one of us living on a cattle ranch.

Those rats may have pleased the cat, but they were unwelcome co-inhabitants of the house. My mother tried everything to get rid of them. The floors were concrete, and they would literally bore up through them. I remember her pouring a kettle of hot water down one of these holes. It did not stem the tide. They were there first, and they were going to stay. Hell, we did not even speak the local language. They probably did. Most likely, though, it was French – another foreign import.

These rats had voracious appetites. There was an extra building in which we stored some furniture, and they chewed the legs off of these. Not the whole leg, I would imagine, but enough to significantly alter their design. I think that is why my mother hated them. She was not afraid of them. There was little she was afraid of. But I did sleep at night with a burning wick floating on a cork in oil beside my bed, under the assumption that the rats, like Dracula, were not fond of the light. It seemed to work.

We also had one American neighbor on the property with a child much younger than me. I remember the woman frantically chasing a rat around her son's bedroom with a broom. She eventually beat it to death, bloodying the walls. Never doubt a woman's spirit in defending her child. Her husband was at work, so he missed the show. We had come in answer to her calls for help, but she took care of the matter. You could not pay me enough to be a rat in a child's bedroom, if he had a healthy mother like that one.

We lived in this place most of the time I was in Morocco. Towards the end we moved to an apartment on the edge of town. I had a little dog then, and there were workmen building something next door. They apparently had chickens running about, and the dog would be found occasionally, or perhaps often, munching on one on our door mat. So the dog had to go.

We had a cat around that time too. I tied a cardboard box to the cat once, and it took off across a neighboring field and disappeared over a wall, box and all. It did eventually get free of the box and died in the winter, sleeping on top of a warm truck engine until someone started the engine and the fan put an end to its dreams. As for the box episode, I guess I was curious and underestimated the intensity of the reaction. It is after all, human curiosity which has transformed the world, not always for the better.

Our preparations for leaving Morocco were interesting. My mother had never learned to drive until that time, and we were

My Early Years in Europe, Africa and Asia

headed for Germany. So she bought a second hand convertible, and we headed for Algeria on a test run. Algeria is where the Sahara is. It heated the plastic back window until it turned black and exploded. The car became known by the air police on the base as "the blue bullet." But she got no tickets because she worked in the legal office.

George Lowell Tollefson

Germany

Shortly after the excursion to Algeria, we loaded up with cases of military-ration chocolate candy bars and headed for the ferry to cross over the Mediterranean to Spain. Passing by the Rock of Gibralter was interesting for the simple reason that it is a famous rock. In Southern Spain we headed out with the car. Throughout most of the trip through Spain my mother was dreading Madrid because there was a huge, busy, traffic circle in the middle of the big city which she would have to pass through. I do not think she had had much experience with traffic circles.

In the south of Spain I was disappointed because it was still relatively arid like Morocco, and I wanted green. We stopped at a bodega of some sort. It was surrounded by dry weeds, nothing else around, and an old woman came out to greet us. She looked as dry as the weeds. That is not a nice thing to say, especially since I must look like that now. We got whatever my mother was after and continued on our way.

I must have slept through much of the drive that day, but I do remember the traffic circle in Madrid. It was very big and very busy. To this day I hate traffic circles, but my mother made it through alright. A traffic circle is a lazy engineer's stoplight.

We crossed through the Pyrenees and drove along the Riviera, both French and Italian, headed for Switzerland. It

My Early Years in Europe, Africa and Asia

was in the heart of Nice that we had an accident, my mother's first, soon to be followed by another in the Swiss Alps. Nice was very trafficy that day. Cars, buses everywhere. In the midst of all these distractions, a bus stopped in the middle of the street. We were passing it in the lane on the right. It disgorged a kid about my age who ran around the bus into our lane, and the edge of the bumper on our car hit him, knocking him to the curb. He was not hurt, other than a few bruises, but we were, after all, "rich Americans." So we were in for some trouble.

But fortunately a French woman, who had been married to an American, witnessed the incident from her balcony. She came to our rescue, affirming the fact that it was not my mother's fault. It took about a week to clear that up, during which time we stayed in Nice. I remember the gooseberry and currant bushes growing thickly inside the gate where we stayed. They were lush, but not so the beach. It was on the other side of the road, and I went down to see it. It was made up of small pebbles, not sand.

I was a very stereotypical type in those days and wanted things to be according to imagination. When they were not, I was disappointed. Come to think of it, most of life has been like that. Imagination and life make strange bedfellows. This sort of thing is probably also the cause of a good many human problems. We want to make not only God but the world in our image, and what an image it is! No wonder things turn out so crazy.

Ah, but Switzerland was nice: cool, mountainous, and dangerous. The hairpin turns were truly the latter. And the blue bullet was a bullet. It zipped along those mountain roads, until it did not quite make one of the turns. My mother applied the brakes, and we skidded to the cliff edge, one back wheel going over it. I looked out the rear side window. It was a long way down there. Rocky too and quite sheer in descent. We sat there for a moment while my mother collected her wits. Then she hit the gas peddle and pulled back onto the road. We continued on our way. I had an extra chocolate bar.

We stopped for the night at an inn. It was wonderful. All dark woodwork and paneling inside. There was a sliding panel between the kitchen and the dining area. The food came through that. Upstairs the sleeping arrangements were a big bed covered with an absolutely weightless feather quilt, which turned out to be quite warm. I placed my box of sand beatles on the night stand, and my mother said they kept her awake during the night because they sounded like rain on a tin roof. They kept scratching the sides of the box, trying to get out. But I do not recall our ever having experienced a tin roof until we were in the Philippines. My mother pointed out the annoyance, but she did not make me discard the beatles. She understood a child's need for inarticulate friends, though they probably did not consider me a friend.

We eventually got to Germany: Spangdahlem Air Base in the south of the country near Bitburg. It is a rainy area, cold in winter, and near where the Battle of the Bulge was fought in the second world war. The forests are damp and incredibly dense, full of wild boars, which the airmen liked to hunt from high stands up in the trees on their days off. Children were

My Early Years in Europe, Africa and Asia

forbidden to go into the forest because of the boars, but of course that did not keep us out of it.

This was the only time we ever lived on base, since there were apparently no available accommodations in the small town nearby. All I remember about that town were the interesting gadgets in some of the shops: cuckoo clocks and various tin figurines surrounding candles. The figures would turn when the candle was lit.

A nine-year-old child's interests are somewhat limited. I am sure there must have been certain accommodations for the single GIs. There were everywhere else. We were quartered in an apartment building, fourth floor. It backed up to the dark and forbidden wonders of the forest. We, the kids, spent a lot of time in that forest when it was not raining. But then it seemed it was always raining. The only relief from the rain was the frozen mud in the winter. That hurt your knees if you fell on it.

Once during the summer I got stuck in the mud. Up to my knees in it. I could not get out. I became frantic. A German workman from a nearby building project came and pulled me out. Otherwise I might have been there for the rest of my life, which would have been short. That was how I saw it.

Now the forest, that was different. It was gorgeously mysterious. We, the kids, built forts in it and sledded in it in winter. It sloped down a steep hill, so that made sledding wild, avoiding the trees, not always successfully. At one point a couple of kids and I were on a sled that went over a big, hidden rock which sent us airborne into a big tree. Boy, did that hurt. But it did not keep us out of the woods.

George Lowell Tollefson

Germany is a beautiful country – naturally, since it is densely forested in places. The forests and the swamps were two of the things that made it so difficult for the Romans to bring the Germanic tribes under control. The other was a lack of cities and towns. Not much different in the latter case from Afghanistan today. But then nations never learn. They do not mind making mistakes, especially when politicians can expend lives not their own on their various adventurous projects.

We started out in our fourth-floor apartment with a very young housekeeper, a dog, and a cat. I am not sure where the cat came from. It spent most of its time hiding between blankets in the hall closet. The dog was a pedigree wire-haired fox terrier. For some reason it urinated regularly in the apartment, probably because I never walked it.

This was one of the many things that infuriated the young housekeeper. But she could not take it out on the dog, since the dog did not understand German. It was a foreigner in its own country. So she took it out on me. I also had a bratty friend who would come over and make life hell for her. So she beat me across the back. This is why the cat would disappear between blankets in the closet. It was not sticking around to defend anyone.

The housekeeper was missing three fingers from one hand. This was a result of a bomb fragment during the war. Her presence in our apartment was apparently due to an interest in catching the eye of a young GI. But this ambition was cut short when my mother found out about the beatings. She fired the housekeeper.

My Early Years in Europe, Africa and Asia

The next one was an older, white-haired lady, who lived on a farm in a nearby incredibly green, beautiful valley tucked on all sides between hills. There were housekeeper's rooms on the top floor of our building, but she went home at night. She had a grandson about my age. I remember playing catch with him at the farm. We had been invited there because she and my mother became friends.

I lack proper depth perception, so I have always been poor at catching a baseball. So, stumbling backwards in an unsuccessful attempt to do so, I fell into a haystack near the house. The hay was mixed with human manure as fertilizer for the fields. I will not describe the result. But there are often compensations for certain types of misfortune. I was served a slice of German cheesecake in the shadowy cool innards of the house. The lights must not have been on. Hence the shadowy effect. A great thing, for all my focus was on the delectable dessert. The cheesecake was paradise in the opinion of my taste buds. They howled with delight.

Now, as an old man I cannot eat dairy products, not to mention a number of other things. Alas, my animal nature drops away, while I cling to whatever mental life there is. That must be why old people are considered wise. They have not got much else to work with. So they concentrate on what they have left. Of course, there is the matter of experience too. The world beats you down into a kind of wistful submission. You talk to yourself and hobble along, and people take you for either wise or crazy. Maybe there is not much difference between the two.

George Lowell Tollefson

When we left Germany, we gave the dog to the housekeeper. Since it had papers, I am sure she was delighted. And out on that farm there was plenty of room and freedom to urinate. This dog had a curious habit while it was with us. It would go out onto the balcony, climb over the surrounding guard rail, and walk along the outer edge of the brick wall that supported the rail. Four stories up. Yet it never fell. Insanity and bravado are close cousins.

Speaking of the balcony, there was a violent thunderstorm one night with a good wind. The wind blew something into the living room that I have never seen before or since. It was a ball of interacting lightning bolts. They spun around and around in the room and then disappeared. We closed the balcony door after that. I do not know why it was open in the first place. The wild outdoors in some cases can be a place of forbidding terrors. That is when the warm interiors of human habitations can be very nice.

Of course, the wildest thing on earth is the human heart. So no guarantees there. There might be one or two of those in the room, and you are shut in with them. The greatest human terror I recall at that time was my raucous friend who infuriated the first housekeeper. At one point I was sent on a class trip to Holland, where I purchased a cheap knife. My mother told me before I left that she was going to give me a nice one, but I must not have believed her. When I got home and she discovered my error, she unveiled a beautiful hunting knife originally meant for me and gave it to my friend. That stung, but I bore it as stoically as I could.

My Early Years in Europe, Africa and Asia

Maybe this incident had something to do with the fact that I was not with my friend on his fateful day. His own family was moving out, no doubt heading for a new duty assignment. A big tractor-trailer was being filled with their household goods, and the kid was playing around the truck, as he should not have been. He was often doing what he should not do. At any rate, when the mover/driver got into his cab and started the engine, he did not see the kid behind him, playing on the hitch fastening the trailer to the tractor. As he pulled out, the boy fell under the wheels of the trailer and was crushed to death.

A lesson in the virtues of appropriate behavior. I never forgot it, even if I did not always heed it. I am a hard case, like all the rest of humankind. I learn lessons and follow them when they are convenient. Otherwise, I dabble on the edges of forbidden lunacy. But I have never climbed on any big trucks. It is those direct, poignant lessons that stay with you. They remain so vivid in the mind, nothing ever removes them.

Two other things I want to mention briefly. Strawberry hunting was quite memorable. You do it on the edges of the forest, where the sun breaks through. Delicious. Another unforgettable thing was visiting a castle and descending into the damp and dripping torture room. There really was such a thing. A place to stretch people out and make them taller, etc.

The human race has always been wonderfully creative. It is those animal traits in all of us that keep the pot of interest boiling. Never a dull interlude. We can always come up with something that will jack your eyelids open and set your heart to pounding. We are truly a creative species. Always have been and damn proud of it, if you ask most people.

That is why our visit to Cologne should be no surprise. The part of the city we passed through had been heavily bombed ten years before and was still in its modified condition. There were apartment buildings with large parts of the front wall missing – and people living in them.

But there is one other thing I want to mention. It concerns a GI who had been there (in Spangdahlem) during the war. He was in the Army then, a lieutenant, a platoon leader. His platoon had been ambushed in the general area where we were and his men wiped out, leaving him the only survivor.

After the war, he transferred over to the Air Force when the latter was separated from the Army. By some quirk of fate he was sent back to Spangdahlem. That was bad enough for the sake of unpleasant memories. But fate is a strangler vine. It goes all the way. The man who picked up his trash once a week was a German who had been in the unit that ambushed his platoon.

This led to heavy drinking on the part of our former lieutenant, who now had a wife and two daughters, one my age and another two years older. The adults were friends of my mother, so we visited them on occasion. The drinking caused problems, and he was busted down to airman second class from whatever rank he had been holding. But did the Air Force have enough sense to realize he needed to be posted somewhere else? No, of course not. What does that have to do with being rough and ready for war?

Ah, specialists. We have them everywhere. In fact, over time our universities have become job training centers creating cartloads of highly trained specialists who can think about nothing outside their fields. Nor should they. There is no remuneration for that, and that is why it takes a football team to bring alumni back to the alma mater. There is nothing about the intellectual environment to impress them, other than a little posing while they were students. The aftereffects of that quickly evaporate.

George Lowell Tollefson

Tokyo, Japan

Well, we did leave Germany after about a year. We were headed for Japan, but we took the long route that crossed the United States. Good to be back, but only for a flash. Mom was a seasoned traveler. We stopped in Washington, DC, and took time out to visit the Walkers out in Franconia. My beloved tree was gone. There was a big apple tree in the backyard that we had loved to climb in, but they had cut it down. Given its size, it must have been old. Old things become weakened and obsolete. Better not think about that, at least until I get this thing written.

I had had a close friend there named Philip, but he wanted nothing to do with me now that I had become tainted with travel. Perhaps he thought I had an African viper hidden in my shirt. After our country visit, we returned to Washington and went to the Seventh Day Adventist Church there. It is their headquarters. My mother was a nominal Adventist and wanted me properly baptized. They had a small pool in the church, and there they attempted to drown me. I survived, much to my amazement, and we went on.

We crossed the country and ended up somewhere. I do not know where. But I do remember the scene. It was a nursing home of some kind, and that is where my old grandmother (great grandmother) was staying. She had become severely

My Early Years in Europe, Africa and Asia

demented and thought my mother (her daughter and granddaughter) was her sister.

In her little room she was tearing pieces of paper into tiny bits and depositing them on her bed. I do not know why, but it must have been sufficiently entertaining. Her dementia had apparently developed slowly because, after my mother left home to go to Washington at the age of twenty, Adelaide's (that was her name) lawyer/accountant wiped out her holdings.

He took it all. We – all her descendants – became lower middle class as a result. Well, why not? We were anyway. As for the lawyer/accountant, people never seem to understand that the greed laissez-faire capitalism breeds spills over into the social milieu. It corrupts the morals of the whole nation.

From there we went on to visit my aunt (great aunt) in Van Nuys, California, then a suburb of Los Angeles. We also visited my true grandmother and step-grandfather in Hollywood. Grandpa Si was a fine, working-class gentleman who spent his retirement years watching the local kids play baseball.

After this visit, we flew to Japan. The flight over was different from jet travel today. We often flew below the clouds, and you could see the whitecaps on the ocean. You also got a lecture on how to use water wings, a rather useless detail nowadays. Those old prop jobs also had the disadvantage of not being well pressurized. I used to double over in pain on takeoff and landing.

East Asia is a long ways away for the US to be so interested in it. But I spent my preteen and teen years up to the age of seventeen there and a few years later fought in the war in Vietnam. In spite of the war, I came to love the whole area.

We went to the Tokyo area first. My mother worked at Tachikawa Air Base as a court reporter and as a protocol assistant. She worked for the commanding general as a protocol assistant because, though he already had a protocol officer, the officer did not know the details of protocol, and my mother did.

Oddly enough, we were only there three months. During that time we lived off base (naturally) outside Tokyo and within sight of Mount Fuji. The old volcano is beautiful. It is a perfect cone and snow capped. No wonder the Japanese love it. It just needs to remain inactive. There are a lot of people in the Tokyo area. There and on the southern island of Kyushu is where most of the people are.

I had a dog of some sort while we lived in that apartment. It was a female, and it adopted a litter of kittens while we were there. Some local person had discarded them near our habitation in the hope an American would take pity on them. But, alas, it was the dog who exhibited the humanity.

Such is the strange nature of events when you let them wind on under their own power. Fate is an orb weaver spider spinning webs of inscrutable mystery and sometimes beauty. That is all I remember about that dog. I do not even remember what it looked like. But that is enough to remember.

My Early Years in Europe, Africa and Asia

The Philippines: Preadolescence

Well, we only lasted three months there. I do not know why. I presume my mother had an opportunity to move on and could not resist it. No moss ever grew under her feet, though we did remain in the next place for four and a half years, where I progressed from a relatively innocent kid to a not so admirable teenager. The place we came to was Clark Air Base in the Philippines. I will always remember it with fondness, though the base authorities will not likely remember me in the same way, if any of them are still around to do so, and I doubt that.

The Philippines had been an American colony from eighteen ninety-eight to nineteen forty-six, when we graciously gave them their independence on our Fourth of July. Why we could not have at least let them have their independence on a day of their own choosing and of historical significance for them, I do not know. At any rate, our presence there was still quite heavy at the time of my sojourn in country.

Needing company, I brought a turtle with me on the plane. I had it in a box in the passenger cabin of the aircraft, and I do not know what it thought of the pressure changes. It was not very talkative. At first, we lived temporarily – very shortly, probably a few weeks – on base in women's housing. Most of the people there were single school teachers for the dependents' school.

George Lowell Tollefson

During our short stay, I think my turtle took a nose dive off the upper floor of the complex. It was composed of two stories and designed with an outside upper walkway like a cheap motel. Anyway, I never saw the turtle again. I would say that by now, sixty-eight years later, the Philippines could be full of turtles like mine. But I do not think turtles are often in the habit of practicing parthenogenesis. Apparently, that practice is limited to rabbits, some fish, and people. But the Philippines is full of animals, so I was not at a loss at finding others a little later, though not turtles. They have dull personalities.

I soon ended up in Baguio. It is up in the mountains north of Clark Air Base. It is an incredibly beautiful place, cool and pine forested. Quite a change from the jungle and rice paddy infested lowlands. Baguio is a resort area, and there was an American facility there for that purpose. But I ended up in a private school run by some Protestant church. I spent only a month there before my mother pulled me out. I lived in a barracks with other kids up to the age of sixteen. There was little supervision, and the older kids bullied the younger ones.

At one point I must have given out some information which was found to be inconvenient, so my head was stuck into a toilet and I was instructed that I had better not do that again. The lessons of life come thick and fast when you are young and tender. Well, I must have shaped up to the required expectations because I soon found myself on a journey of exploration.

Several of the older kids, including, I believe, the sixteen-year-old head plunger, slipped away from the school for a day in the woods. They took me with them, as I clearly needed

My Early Years in Europe, Africa and Asia

instruction in the finer points of life. We found a river, and everyone except me went for a swim. I could not swim, so I was happy to stay ashore on the rocky river bank. But this would not do. "You see that rope bridge up there?" I was told. There was a narrow, rather spooky looking, fragile bridge high above us crossing the steep canyon through which the river flowed. "Do you want to cross it?" "No." "Well then, swim." "But I do not know how." "No problem, we will help you."

So out into the current I went, sitting on someone's shoulders. As he proceeded toward the middle of the stream, the water deepened. Soon the water was over his head, and I was up there scared as hell. Needless to say, he could not remain in that position long, so he swam out from under me. Fortunately, another kid extended a long pole out toward me from the bank. I grabbed hold of it and was pulled ashore. My first swimming lesson. When my mother came for a visit, I may have informed her of my adventures and was pulled out of the school. I was ten years old at the time, though I turned eleven within a few weeks.

Back in the general vicinity of Clark Air Base, we moved into a house in Balibago, an off-base American housing area just outside the main gate to the base. The house we lived in was electrified. If a Filipino came by for some reason and leaned on the door jam to express his purpose, he would receive a severe jolt and be knocked out into the yard. If the television set was turned on – there was little reason for doing so – what looked like fire balls would descend from the ceiling. It was not until later that we discovered the cause. The house had a tin roof, and the power cable was laying on the roof. Perhaps it was a bit frayed.

At any rate, I began my animal accumulation process here. I obtained a little brown puppy. I kept it, probably on a rug, beside by bed. But it did not last long. It died of hook worm infestation. Shortly after that, a Filipino man arrived after dark in the rain with a little black puppy. It was female. So, being quite imaginative, I named it Blackie. It was to be with us throughout our four and a half years in the Philippines.

As for the house, we were only there for a couple of months. It was during the monsoon season. So, one day while we were away, it rained until everything was flooded: the dirt road, surrounding yards, everything. Blackie, now chained outside, was in desperate straits. She found a nearby overturned bucket and was standing on it when the neighbors found her. They rescued her and returned her to us when we came home, informing us of the high waters, which had by then receded.

The reason I had these dogs is that there were goats grazing in the neighboring fields. One of them had two kids, so I appropriated them and brought them into my yard. This was not to be allowed. It is called stealing. So that is why I got the dogs, after I returned the kids to their mother. But it was not the first such instance. In Morocco there was a spotted dog hanging about the property of the citrus farm. She had a litter of pups, and, believing her to be a stray, I saw no reason why I should not have one. When the landlord found out, he was furious. It was many years before I could understand why he was so upset. Apparently, the dog was a Bedouin-Israeli

My Early Years in Europe, Africa and Asia

breed, quite expensive. Well, I just had to have animals. It was an obsession, probably the result of not having siblings and moving about so much.

But I was also fascinated with living things – other sources of conscious awareness. Of course, I did not know then that I would some day develop a philosophy positing consciousness as prior to the material. It became for me a necessary reversal, wherein the material emanates from universal awareness, somewhat like the physical universe coming out of a singularity as a result of the Big Bang. But it is not the same thing. Nevertheless, it is interesting to posit same kind of consciousness within the singularity, which then emits a content for that consciousness.

However, hanging any philosophy on the fragile framework of a science is impermissible. Science is a product of imagination and intellect. And though philosophy is as well, it is also a concerted attempt to reach well beyond the evidence of the senses and the circumscribed resources of imagination. It can only do so on the crutches of sensory evidence and its resulting imaginative constructs, but, nevertheless, it strains with all its might to obtain a peek at what lies beyond. That is a tall order, but a necessary one.

Religions do the same thing as a kind of picture philosophy. Philosophy attempts to get beyond the pictures, which are always somewhat fabricated and to that extent false, by concealing its imaginations within concepts, thus giving them the dignity of detached abstractions. But humanity is always limited to its experiences and those hidden impulses which attempt to reshape them in the interests of a deeper understanding. It is the hidden impulses which are of true concern. But how does one explore the doings of consciousness itself without the assistance of its content?

Our next habitation was a house on the other side of Angeles. True to form, this one turned out not to have electricity. I do not know why. The house was wired, but at eleven I was not in on the details. Nevertheless, no electricity notwithstanding, we were there for a short while, and, among other things, I obtained a pet monkey. Mean bugger. It bit you with teeth like a human's, which means they did not as a rule penetrate. They just hurt like hell.

There was a barrio nearby – a Filipino village – and the monkey drew kids from there. We had a chain link fence around the yard, which was six or eight feet tall. You know how it is with kids. I remember it as sixteen feet tall. At any rate, the barrio kids were fascinated by the monkey, and unfortunately their response was to tease it by poking long sticks through the fence at it. It was fastened around the waist, and that was attached to a long, light chain secured to an outer post of the carport. I do not know if the monkey got loose or the chain length was sufficient, but one day it went over the fence and bit a young girl on the face so she bled. Rabies is a serious threat in the Philippines, or at least it was then, so the incident created quite a ruckus.

It was shortly after that we moved again. I do not remember the electrical problem ever being solved while we were there. Well, who needs electricity? There is always the great outdoors. There was a sanitarium at one end of the neighborhood. I believe it was for tuberculosis. That would have made my

My Early Years in Europe, Africa and Asia

mother nervous. There was plenty of that in the Philippines at the time.

They had a flock of white turkeys on the grounds, and they appeared to be as imbecilic as most domestic turkeys. They probably had to have special instructions on how to peck the ground when they were young. They must have insects and what not to flavor the meat, give it a gamey taste, and they have got to have pebbles to grind the stuff. Grasshoppers and beetles have stiff wing carapaces. But I do not know if they were eaten at the sanitarium. The turkeys, I mean. Certainly, insects were plentiful. Other American kids and I hunted grasshoppers in the tall grass by gathering bunches of it and swatting down the grasshoppers with the bunches as they flew up to get away from us. They were colorful under their wings, bright orange and yellow.

Soon we were out of there. We moved to a neighborhood on the opposite side of Tarlac Road from Balibago. Tarlac Road was the main road running north and south through the area, extending onward to the town of Angeles and beyond. The road itself was lined with small businesses: garages, tire repair shops and the like, just as the main gate to the air base was lined with small stands selling black market American cigarettes. They were just a hundred yards or so from the gate – outside it, of course.

Every now and then the base commander would change the scrip. Scrip was a kind of military play money designed to substitute for dollars. It did not slow the black market, even with the frequent changes. When the changes came, local people would arrive with bucket loads of scrip, hoping to find some way of exchanging it for the latest fashion in play money. The panic was clearly etched on their faces.

This new neighborhood was, of course, a smaller duplicate of Balibago. It may well have been considered part of Balibago, but it had a different name: Mountain View, I think – unless that was the name of the previous neighborhood closer to Angeles. But there was a view from it of a saddle-topped mountain which was rumored to be inhabited by Huks. Huk is short for Hukbalahap, the name of a communist guerilla movement in Central Luzon Island. They were active and were rumored to slip into populated areas now and then to create mayhem. The story was that they had pointed ears, so they were not hard to recognize. I never encountered them.

When I arrived home from school the day we moved, I discovered the monkey was not at the new house. My mother had discreetly gotten rid of him. No real loss. I remember an episode at the former house where I had some frogs in a container, and the monkey ran over, grabbed a frog, and quickly climbed up a rain spout conduit on the side of the house. He got far enough up to be out of reach, then stopped, bit the head off the frog and munched away.

Well, so much for that frog. But, as is plain to see, my fondness for the monkey was not at a high point by the time of the move. There were other interests. I had a couple of white farm ducks, at least one of which I must have gotten from a friend named Robert. I do not remember knowing him in the countryside, but I do remember visiting him often after he moved onto the base. We were good friends. You see, I was allowed free admittance to the base, since my mother worked

My Early Years in Europe, Africa and Asia

there. We just could not live there. It was just as well. I had a lot more interesting adventures in the countryside. Certainly better memories.

Now, I also had a new friend in the latest new neighborhood. She was a girl several years younger than me, named Alison. She was blond and mean as sin toward her one pet duck, a dark-feathered drake. It was a duckling when we first met, but it grew up fast into a rather large creature. She would daily slap its head back and forth with both hands, so, when it was grown, it had developed a hateful personality, more in size and temperament like a goose.

When grown, which only took a few months, it would fly over to my house and land in the backyard, ready to court my two ducks, who were both females. If anyone, particularly the housekeeper, came into the yard, it would fly up and nip her with its bill. That hurt, so she would confront it with a broom. But it was a considerable nuisance at that. So Alison clipped its wings.

We lived about a block apart, and what did it do? It walked down the dirt road between our houses and somehow could get over my fence. Problem not solved. I think now that Alison must have clipped both wings equally, so the beast could still become airborne enough to scale the wall. But the amazing thing was its willingness to walk the walk for its bit of carnal pleasure.

There are people like that too. Their minds never reach out further than the end of – you know what I mean. The world has always been like that, but it seems to be particularly like that now. Civilization progresses slowly, going round and round in pursuit of flesh, then more abstract goals, then more flesh (lots of that).... Life goes on.

I do have some memories from around that time which I cannot accurately place. One is playing in some farmer's haystacks with other American kids. There must have been a community nearby, and I am sure they were tickled pick to see us messing up their haystacks, or whatever they were.

I also remember being somewhere around there and watching a Filipino boy about my age riding his water buffalo into a water hole to cool it off, I presume, and to get rid of some nagging insects. The water hole was pretty muddy, but the carabao did not mind. To control them, a rope is passed through their nostrils, which is held by the rider like a set of reins. It seems to work well once they are properly trained. But do not mess with them before that.

I also remember getting into a fight with such a boy, perhaps the same one. He and his dad, I presume, were passing down a dirt road (the neighborhood roads were all dirt) in a wooden cart, transporting something. In my childish audacity, I climbed aboard. That resulted in the boy and I tumbling off the cart onto the road in an ear-pulling wrestling match. I do not remember how it ended or who won. What possessed me to do that in the first place, I do not know. So if I lost, I deserved it, but I think it was a draw.

I have no sense of why we soon moved out of that house. It may have had to do with the fact that the next house was much nicer. Its outer walls were a thin sheet of plywood, and that was all that was needed in that climate. It had a large living room, a kitchen, and a small servant's room off the kitchen. I

My Early Years in Europe, Africa and Asia

am not sure if there were two bathrooms or one. The one I remember was at one end of the living room next to my bedroom door. Another may have been in the master bedroom, also off the big living room. The servant's room may also have had a separate toilet compartment.

After we had been there awhile, the housekeeper was not allowed to clean my room. I kept it in a trashed condition, which included several Negrito barbed arrows shot into the walls. Negritos are an indigenous race of black pygmy peoples in Southeast Asia. They were employed on Clark Air base as guards at night, since they were considered especially trustworthy, probably because they were a discriminated minority in the Philippines and did not like the Malaysian Filipinos.

The new house also had a double yard, so there was plenty of space for my expanding animal collection, mostly chickens. There were other houses, one behind and one beside it, and open fields stretched out on the other side and the front. These were usually occupied by herds of domestic carabao and goats. The location was the large American neighborhood we had originally lived in, called Balibago.

Up the street, always a dirt road, was a sari-sari store, which sold beer, cigarettes, and other small items. These little stores were located strategically throughout the neighborhood. Also along some of the streets were picture sellers selling paintings on velvet. The paintings usually featured the saddleback mountain I mentioned, and might have a nipa hut or a man on a carabao in a rice field. The paintings were not sold in a shop. They were usually displayed on the ground at some strategic corners.

Other peddlers wandered through the neighborhood, as well as some beggars. Americans, it must be recalled, were considered rich almost everywhere. My mother was always concerned about the beggars because she was convinced some of them might have tuberculosis. So when one of them showed up, she gave him something and shooed him away.

Another thing she always did when we lived abroad was keep detailed records of receipts of any kind of payments, like rent. She said that, if you did not, the rent, or utilities, or whatever, was likely to be collected twice. This gradually became true even in the United States as time passed and we became more like the rest of the world with which we were in so much contact.

Gone are the days of the handshake business deal. This is not all a result of foreign exposure. Once a nation reaches peak economic expansion and the people begin to feel financially squeezed, they resort to taking shortcuts in moral expression. No one wants to be the sucker who did not see the changes coming and was the only one who let advantages slip.

This new house – it had only recently been built – was owned by an American married to a Filipino woman. He had been transferred stateside, but intended to return to that house for his retirement. It was nice. It had concrete floors stained barnyard red like an ox blood dirt floor. The walls in the living room were different shades of blue. My mother did not like this. But there it was. There were screens on all the windows, and during flying ant season, they became clotted with flying ants, literally so you could not see out of them. There were

My Early Years in Europe, Africa and Asia

many insects of every description, and many of them wanted to try out the house.

Fortunately we had geckos. They shared the house with us and usually confined themselves to the ceilings where they would scamper about on their adhesive padded feet in search of insects gathered near the lights at night. They sang loudly in the evenings, but you got used to it. Now and then you would find one of their eggs on a windowsill, and they had tails that detached easily in a crisis. I once read a book describing them as falling onto your dinner plate, but that never happened. They were agile creatures and not prone to foolish maneuvers. They lived mostly up there. We lived in contact with the floor. Shared space, since there was enough to go around.

In the tropics you make these accommodations, whether you want to or not. Another interesting creature was the giant water bug. These were truly giants, as much as six inches long and two or more inches wide, shaped like a boat. One rainy season they were so thick on the ground you could not get about without walking on them. They smelled like overripe bananas. There were also large horned rhinoceros beetles. I collected these in my early years there. I also made a dart gun with needles or pins, strands of bamboo off a stiff type of broom, and a rubber band. Pretty efficient. I hunted skink lizards with it.

Speaking of hunting, I loved birds, so I hunted them in the tall grass of the surrounding fields. I did not want to harm them. I wanted to collect them. So I went out and hid in the grass armed with a slingshot our later gardener helped me make from a Y-joint of branched tree wood, strips of inner tube, and something leather for the pouch to hold the stone.

The bird I hunted would do a song and dance over the field, soaring and diving like a lark, no doubt to impress a female (how much living energy is expended on courting rituals?). Unfortunately, these were insect eaters, so they did not fare very well on the diet of seeds I gave them in my ignorance. They usually perished in a few days. Of course, there was the injury from the stone too.

At any rate, I was proud of my cunning in the grass and accuracy with the slingshot, but I have long since been ashamed of my cruel ignorance. What did I know? What do I know now about such birds? How much unnecessary cruelty is committed out of such ignorance in both children and adults? But then, it is a brutal world, as war would later teach me. Not all of it can be avoided.

As for the bird, I am not sure if I only took one or several. Too long ago. Nevertheless, birds were my obsession. Their quick, nervous ways are an ultimate display of conscious awareness, and I could never get enough of it. One of the peddlers who would come through our neighborhood, plodding along on clogs cut from old tires, or barefoot, carrying a long bamboo pole over one shoulder with cages containing and not containing birds slung from it, was a delight to me. I would rush out to him and, with whatever small change I had, purchase a bird or two: Java rice birds and little green parrots no bigger than the rice birds.

The rice birds had a strong, finch beak like a grossbeak, and their bite was not at all pleasant. Nor were they averse to

My Early Years in Europe, Africa and Asia

delivering such a bite as they were being transferred to a cage for delivery into my hands. But the bird seller put up with it. It was his line of business. As it turned out, the parrots almost always died within a few days, and their disease often spread to my other birds, including ducks and chickens.

But I was not a quick learner in such matters. I could never get enough birds, especially the chickens. I do not know how many of them I accumulated. Plenty. I would grab one of my poor (I presumed unsuspecting) mother's tools and be off to a barrio (village) to trade for chicks. Of course, they lived free, wandering under the nipa huts, and I had to capture them myself. The brainy little buggers would head for the nearest clump of hairy bamboo. The hairs on the bamboo would cut into my flesh and leave stinging scratches all over my arms. It stung like almighty because I would be sweaty from the tropical heat.

I did other things, like outrunning monsoons. The rain would come down in a straight, flat sheet. You could clearly see it approaching from afar off. I remember seeing one when I was just coming home to Balibago. I was still outside the neighborhood when I got off the Green Bus. The buses on base had different names based on colors, and the one that went off base was the Green Bus. My house was deep within the neighborhood, so I made a run for it. Unfortunately, I had to turn several corners, and that changed my angle to the approaching wall of rain. Panic. Too late. I made a turn and ran smack into it. I was instantly soaked and arrived home like a wet gunnysack.

George Lowell Tollefson

Everything in the tropics seems abrupt, even when announced, like the sheet of rain. It said to me: "Here I am. I am coming, and there is nothing you can do about it." Okay, so I got wet. What does a kid care? I changed clothes and continued my activities. One of these was fishing for tadpoles. Pollywog heaven. Big bullfrog tadpoles and smaller leopard frog tadpoles.

Our neighborhood was surrounded by rice paddies because that is what it had once been. Near the borders were these big pools, or puddles, full of frog offspring. All you had to do was reach in there with something and scoop them up. Unfortunately, they were not the only residents in those dark pools. Concealed beneath their muddy waters were also leeches. When I would pull my arm out, they would be stuck to it. I would brush them off. A little blood, not much. But that was the price of these amphibian pets.

My neighborhood friends and I also took to riding water buffalo. It was easy to catch them in the fields around my house and climb up. Now, the problem is knowing what to do when you get up there. You cannot ride them like a horse. A carabao has a very broad back. So it is like sitting on a table. Eventually I discovered by watching Filipino boys ride them that you fold your knees back, and that secures your balance.

But at this early stage, my young friends and I did not know this. We would just climb up, and my dog, Blackie, who was usually out there with us – mating with every dog on earth if she was in season – would start barking at the carabao and set it to running. Often the whole herd joined it in headlong flight. Of course, they had to jump over the ditches separating the

My Early Years in Europe, Africa and Asia

fields. I remember two of us being mounted on one and barely hanging on, until it crossed a ditch. We both fell into the ditch, laughing and wetting our pants.

The secret to water buffalo rodeoing is to find one that has a rope through its nose. Otherwise, it might not be trained, and being charged by one – big, curving horns down and forward – is intimidating. Later in my teens, I and several others encountered a young bull in dense jungle brush, and it charged. We dove off the path in both directions, and the buffalo reached the end of a rope it was tethered to.

There was also another problem with this sport. Those were not our carabao. I remember once being out in those fields and a Filipino boy tending them (they were often unattended) was quite annoyed with my dog chasing the herd. So he started throwing rocks at the dog. In return, I threw rocks at him. In return, he threw rocks at me. Fortunately, both of us had lousy aim, deliberate or otherwise. One last thing we did. Another kid and I rode a carabao up to the outer cinder brick wall of an American house in the neighborhood. The wall was relatively low, and there was a guava tree on the other side of it. The fruit was ready, so we helped ourselves.

Rain on a tin roof sounds like rain on a tin roof. How else would you describe it? The point is, you know just how many drops are falling at any one time. And, of course, in a monsoon it is a tidal wave. Huge ruts and gullies are made in the dirt roads. Slish-slosh as cars pass along them, slipping from side to side. It is a good time to be wearing those clogs made out of old tires. A regular shoe sunk in mud has no life left in it. It dies right there, but still clinging hopelessly to your foot.

George Lowell Tollefson

I should probably mention that my chicken collection kept growing. My mother's tool supply shrank accordingly. She did eventually let me know she was aware of my thievery. I do not remember what the solution was. Naturally, my chickens had to be housed. They already had the annoying habit of going over the back fence into a neighbor's yard. I must have been a pain to a lot of people.

Blackie had pups every seven months. You always knew there would be another litter a couple of months ahead of time because there would be a row of male dogs sitting in front of the gate with erections. Very single minded, like some people. Usually those people with less breeding, so to speak, are the most obvious. Anyway, one of those pups grew up into a kitten killer.

A neighbor – the side one, not the back one – had a litter of kittens. That is to say, their cat had the litter. Cute, I presume, until the dog tore them up. Eyes in one place, other parts in other places. The eyes are much bigger than you would suspect, looking from the outside of a cat's face when they are still in it.

Naturally, the dog had to go. My mother's orders were delivered to our gardener. He came and got the dog from the carport and drug it around to the back of the house. He was carrying a pipe. I stayed on the carport. I heard the loud, hollow crack. End of dog. Lesson: leave a neighbor's cats to their own devices.

Unfortunately, few dogs have ever gotten the hang of this rule. Like people, they think rules are always for others, until the ax falls. It is said that Jonathon Swift was disappointed at

My Early Years in Europe, Africa and Asia

the public reception to *Gulliver's Travels*. He wanted to upset people, not amuse them – cause them to take a hard look at themselves. Instead, they cast a bemused critical eye upon their neighbors, not themselves.

Back to the subject of chickens. Our yard was full of them. Some friends and I had built a clubhouse with our gardener's help. But we were inside it only once. One of them thought we should do a circle jerk, and I dropped the friends, or they dropped me. Who cares for a young prude, such as myself? At any rate, the clubhouse was converted into a two-story chicken coop. To hell with clubhouses.

The chickens would roost in the upper section and nest on the ground in the lower section. Amazingly, I would manage to crawl into this thing. Crowded it was, but I was fascinated with the hatching chicks. Such little, quickened lives coming out of an egg. Often I could not wait. I would hear the peeping chick inside and see the little peck hole in the shell and help it along. I would peel it out of the egg. Well, it was crowded in the bottom of that coop, and I would be sitting there (no doubt in the filth: chickens poop a lot) with my knees up. Once, holding a newly liberated chick up to see it, I dropped it and caught it with my knees. Not good for infant birds. I had to finish it off.

I should mention the succession of housekeepers at our latest house, the one we lived in for the rest of the time we were in the Philippines. We started with a man named Alex. He spent a disproportionate amount of his time standing at the back fence gossiping with the housekeeper on the other side. He did not last long. He was paid to work, not gossip.

George Lowell Tollefson

The next one was a young girl who claimed she was nineteen. My mother judged that she was about sixteen. That made her about five years older than me. But she was a no-nonsense hard worker. She was not only our housekeeper, but our cook. My mother taught her to cook. She learned quickly and did well at it.

There was only one thing at which she did not do well. She refused to use the clothes washing machine. She would not learn how to use it. She washed our clothes at the back door, outside wash basin on a scrub board. She got the job done, so no complaints. But what a lot of unnecessary hard work. She must have been spooked by the machine. She never did use it, and she was with us for the rest of the time we were in country, which was about four years.

She may have been an Igorot from the mountainous, pine-forested region in the northern part of Luzon Island, the island we were on and the administrative center of the country. This would have meant she spoke Ilokano as well. Her careful English quickly improved while she was with us, and she became like an older sister to me.

That means I liked to tease her. I would come out the back door while she was washing clothes and give a nice little yank to one of her pigtails as I ran off. She would let out a complaint and continue with her scrubbing. Once she was cleaning something she used for a kotex pad. I asked her what it was. I really did not know. But she was not amused and told me I did not need to know.

She would eat rice for lunch, and I would tell her she was eating maggots. She did not appreciate this either. Neverthe-

My Early Years in Europe, Africa and Asia

less, in spite of my pranks, we got along well. Many years later, she sent me a card, but, believing my first wife did not want me to respond for some reason, I did not answer it. I have always regretted that.

We also had a "yard boy" during the same period. "Yard boy" is in my opinion a derogatory term for gardener, but it was used by Americans in the Philippines. He is the one who dispatched our errant second-generation dog at my mother's orders. Like Lori, the housekeeper and cook, he was a very good person and was also with us throughout that four years. He was young, maybe late twenties or early thirties, and he had a family. His name was Orley.

At one point, he traded me a couple of guinea pigs for one of Blackie's pups. Her pups were highly prized in that part of the country because of her reputation as an aggressive guard dog. This had resulted from the fact that the garbage men would kick her as a pup when she barked at them as they came to get the garbage. When grown, the tables were turned, and we had to chain her up before they would enter the yard. However, when she was out with me running around in the fields chasing goats or water buffalo, she harmed no one. It was just her yard that was off limits territory. Enter at your peril.

As for the guinea pigs, I kept them in a cage on top of the chicken coop. But I would let them out on the grass once in a while. One day Blackie came careening around the house and mauled one of the guinea pigs before I could stop her. The other one died shortly afterward, possibly from loneliness.

This reminds me of an incident with a recalcitrant rooster. When it rains in that part of the world, it truly rains. So the idea in my mind was that all chickens should get into the coop and out of the rain. Most of them did that day when it began to rain. But the rooster was indifferent to the elements. Perhaps he had some domestic turkey in him. That would be an IQ reducer. That, at any rate, is the way he acted.

I became incensed trying to get him out of the rain. Finally, I picked up a hard rubber ball that belonged to my dog and threw it across the yard at him. Normally, I could not hit the broad side of a barn with a chair two feet from it. But when I am angry things change. I hit the rooster square in the head, and over he went, flopping around on the ground on his head. Boy, did I feel guilty. I think I even prayed. Finally he righted himself and resumed doing nothing about anything. But I did not bother him further. Let the damn thing be a turkey.

Orley came three days out of the week and essentially acted as a handyman. He is the one who taught me how to build the clubhouse/chicken coop. For example, I learned to make door hinges out of strips of leather or rubber inner tube. I learned how to make a simple latch with a stick inserted through it as a way to secure the door. He is also the one who helped me design my slingshot.

The principal thing he did on the job was help Lori scrub and polish the big living room floor once a week. It was not a simple job. The furniture had to be moved, though much of it was made of rattan and therefore light. Still, some of it, such as a large credenza with a separate glassed-in cabinet on top and other individual pieces of furniture in other parts of the room, was made of heavy Nara wood, a kind of mahogany. My mother had these made in Angeles at a cabinetry shop, using money obtained from the sale of commissary groceries on the black market. She said even the colonels did it, so why should she not do it?

The floor itself, as I have mentioned, was a thick slab of concrete that was a good six inches higher coming into the house from the concrete carport. It was stained barnyard red, and this is what they cleaned and polished. Of course, cleaning is cleaning, and I need not describe it. But the polishing was interesting. They did not have a buffer. *They* were the buffer. Orley would slice a coconut shell in half with a bolo (a Filipino machete) and use the halves, one each to himself and Lori. These shells have strong, brushlike fibers, and the brown shell is more than an inch thick. So they would place the half shell on the floor, cut fiber end down, put one foot on top of the rounded end of the shell, and proceed to move it back and forth, eventually over the whole floor. It created a nice shine. Every week.

You can see why Orley was needed. Cleaning and polishing that floor was a big job. But of course he did many other useful things. And, as for animal slaughter rituals, Lori occasionally did that too. We had a white Leghorn pullet that took to jumping up on the charcoal grill on the carport and laying an egg off one end. Splat: a mess to clean up. That went on for awhile, and my mother got fed up with it. Orders were issued. Lori went out and caught the pullet. She took it to a far corner of the large side yard fence and dispatched it by holding on to its head and swinging it rapidly round and round until dead. Though she went to the far corner of the yard, I followed her and observed the ritual. She also had a way of calling the chickens by rapidly vibrating her tongue in a burring sound.

The reason I was so interested in her butchering performance is that I had recently performed an experiment with this young, inexperienced hen (Or so I thought I remembered. It turned out to be a different hen, I believe.) Not being the kindliest person in the world, I shut her up in a wooden box with a wire mesh front. In with her I had placed four or five newly hatched chicks which I had traded for in a nearby barrio. I wanted to see if she would adopt them. So I left them confined that way for about a week. I must have fed them some way, but I do not know how.

She was not happy with the chicks. It was crowded in that box, so they were forced to be snuggled up under her wings and feathers for the most part. She pecked one of them in the eye and blinded it on one side. But after a week or so, I let them out, and amazingly they stayed together. They followed her around like any brood of chicks, and she would keep up a low clucking sound to encourage them and keep them in range. At night they slept under her wings. The adoption was complete.

What interested me was that she did this without the preceding conditions of laying eggs and brooding them on a nest. This taught me that instinctual behavior does not have to follow a programmed sequence. The hen had not brooded any eggs. She was a young pullet and completely inexperienced. I have remembered her for many years as the same hen as the one that met its end for laying eggs on the carport. But now

My Early Years in Europe, Africa and Asia

that I think about it, that does not seem likely. So much for long term memory.

Hell, so much for any memory at all at my age. But I do remember abstractions nicely. I have a penchant for philosophical thought, and I find that such ideas caught up in a web of associations stick in my mind. On the other hand, I hate rote memorization, such as is employed in learning the vocabulary of a foreign language. I fairly easily (not too easily) master the structure of a language but cannot bear learning the vocabulary. It is as boring as it must be for a bird to pick up pebbles for its craw and gizzard. Passing up morsels of food for little stones seems rather disheartening. So much for language study.

My chickens were an eternal fascination to me. Over time, I built up quite a flock, and I had ducks, dogs, cats, small birds, and whatever else I could come up with. I decided one day to demonstrate to my mother the flight of a duck. These were ordinary white farm ducks. Next to the house near the back door was a large, wired-in pen for small birds that was about five feet long, a couple of feet wide, and stood at a height of about four feet. My mother stood at the end near the back door. This was in the relatively narrow backyard. But the side yard extending out from the other end of the five-foot-long bird pen was an entire extra lot. That was where all my chickens and ducks were. Only a few ducks, many more chickens.

I took one of the grown ducks and headed out across the field that extended beyond our side yard fence. I went out to the road beyond and released the duck. The duck flew straight home, going so low to the ground I thought it would not clear the fence. But it did, and it came to a landing on the far end of the top of the bird pen. Its feet were muddy, so it slid across the pen and collided with my mother, slipping muddily down the front of her fresh clean dress. She was not happy, but, as usual, she forgave me on the spot after a few words of shock and went into the house and changed.

My chickens did have chicks, and my ducks did produce a few ducklings. But the ducklings died from what I believed was parrot fever because I was convinced that the little green parrots were responsible for the loss. Some chicks died to, but many made it to adulthood. Those birds that did die I took out into one of the surrounding fields to dispose of them. A goat had died out there in a depression in the ground, and there it lay, rotting away. I would throw the birds in and start a fire. How I kept the fire from spreading I do not recall, but the goats and water buffalo did keep the grass and weeds cropped quite low in that field.

It was all a lesson in life for me. It was very clear that life had its ending and that I was a living form like the rest. But then a child generally feels immortal in spite of the facts. I remember one friend claiming he would never die. I did not go that far. I knew better. But like most people I put thoughts of the end off to a far horizon.

Now that I am old, things look a little different – in fact, irritatingly so. But the irritation has more to do with the increasing physical limitations than with the end. I suppose the gradual physical breakdown helps one to accept the final coup de grace. I will check back on that one a little later, when I know more, which no doubt I will, whether I want to or not.

As I have said before, my interest in the chickens sprang from their nervous liveliness. The liveliness pointedly delineates the fact of consciousness: that miracle of life called awareness. Where is there a greater miracle? Even the purported resurrection of Jesus dims a little beside this fact, since it is simply a resumption of consciousness, if it occurred in the manner usually understood.

So what is consciousness? It seems that most, if not all, philosophers have been avoiding a direct confrontation with this question. When they do sidestep around or near it, they conflate it with reason. But reason is not awareness. It is the content of it. This is why I established my philosophical position directly on this difficult question. What if one began with the fact of consciousness and deduced everything else from it? That would certainly be taking subjectivity (the epistemological approach) a step further. It is a direction that physical science has been traveling anyway with its relativity and quantum mechanics.

But Einstein, at least, would have been the very last to acknowledge the subjectivity in this extreme. He was committed to the separate integrity of nature. So it was my duty in much later years to uphold the lawful order of nature while nevertheless deriving it from awareness. But such an effort is to be found primarily in my books, *The Immaterial Structure of Human Experience*, *The limits of Reason*, and *The Thinking Process*. However, these are, to say the least, not a fit topic for the present narration.

Returning to the subject of chickens, I at one time witnessed a cock fight in my side yard. It took place between one almost fully grown big gray rooster and a much younger red rooster. I was fonder of the red rooster because of his red and gold spangled beauty, but the gray one was admittedly a better singer when he mounted the cinder block wall lining the dirt road at the front of the side yard. His crow was clear and authoritative.

The little red fellow, on the other hand, had much yet to learn. When he attempted a rival display, it was pathetic. It sounded like someone was trying to strangle him. Well, there were a lot of nice hens at stake, even if the red rooster's interest was somewhat pubescent in character. One has to be an upstart at some point to get a foothold in the world. So the competitive displays went on, until finally they resulted in a round of individual combat.

The red rooster, much lighter than the gray one, did not do well. He was roundly defeated. The gray rooster strode off proudly, no doubt to claim a covey of hens, most of them older and wiser than he was. It must have been like claiming a covey of middle-aged mothers. But the little red fellow had lost his bid for such dominance. So he retreated into a row of water plants at the end of the side yard opposite to the cinder block wall. This was where the ducks spent most of their time, wallowing in the damp mud. Hence my mother's experience with the homecoming flight. Lori's wash water ran off in this direction. That is why it was wet.

Here the red rooster sulked over his defeat, until within a few days he died in the manner I had labeled parrot fever. This

My Early Years in Europe, Africa and Asia

is much of the story of life: competition, success or failure, and possible grinding defeat. It gives a sour tinge to much of human existence, since we are not much different from these chickens. The principal human distinction is an enlarged imagination and an occasional, very occasional, use of reason. So occasional is the use of reason that we do not realize just how ridiculous we are most of the time.

Then there is spite, a particular human confection, five parts imagination, no parts reason. Throw in spite, and you have the human milieu. Add nuclear weapons, and God help us. I never did think much of war, having been in one. If you can have rules of war, which are admittedly rarely obeyed, then why not a rule of no war? But clearly that is too much reason and too little ego. The latter is obviously more important.

Never having forgotten the near drowning episode (as I saw it) up in Baguio, I got in the habit about this time of going on base to the pool and teaching myself to swim. I was never much good at it, but I did put a lot of effort into it. The pool was at one end of a park with giant mango trees. These trees were huge. They had probably been there for quite some time. Anyway, I had a tendency to get foot cramps, which turned into leg cramps. So there was a bit of risk in the venture, since I went swimming alone. But there was probably a lifeguard there. I do not remember.

The mango trees remind me of my trek into the Subic jungle at the south end of Luzon. I had a habit of joining the Boy Scouts in the summer for such things and dropping out in the winter. I did not like knot tying and other merit badge projects. So I was a perpetual tenderfoot. One summer we were trucked to the base of the Subic mountains, and from there we hacked our way with bolos through the dense underbrush, including thickets of bamboo of the kind that lacerated your skin, inviting the inevitable sweat to sting like almighty. But we made it to the top before nightfall and set up some tents.

We were above the clouds when we arrived, but, after nightfall, those clouds rose to the plateau we were on and soaked the tents. So we all ended up around a big bonfire trying to stay warm. All through the night we heard calls like whistles, which we thought were men. But they may have been attributable to the gibbons inhabiting the jungle. In the morning, we noticed that the trees on one side of the mountain, looking down from the plateau, were growing out uniformly almost horizontally. Strange.

We hiked to another plateau nearby and attempted to triangulate our position with a compass. I do not remember if that was successful. But I do remember how sheer the drop-off was: hundreds, maybe a thousand feet. But we will not rely upon a kid's perceptions. Suffice it to say, it was a long way down along a straight wall of sheer rock. This plateau was only a small promontory, dropping off in this precipitous manner on three sides. Several of us were crowded into the small space.

Eventually we hiked back down and entered a camp in the jungle below. There we stayed for a few days. It was a campsite already set up, and we slept in a big canvas garrison tent held up by two poles, one at either end. On one of those morn-

My Early Years in Europe, Africa and Asia

ings quite a commotion took place. The campsite was covered with big mango trees like the ones on Clark Air Base, and a troop of gibbons had entered them about dawn. So had a bevy of boar on the ground. The gibbons did not like the boar, so they made a lot of noise and pelted them with mangos. I slept through the whole thing, but, when I finally awoke and went outside the tent, I saw that the ground was covered with mangos. The details of the event I got from others who were more alert than me.

Oh yes. I do not want to forget that there was a threat of a typhoon at home, not at the above time, but in the rainy season. It flooded the city of Manila, so that people were riding down the streets on garbage cans. So we knew it was coming. We brought all of my chickens and other animals into the house and crammed them into the bathroom nearest my bedroom. What a mess. And the typhoon did not come after all.

This, of course, brings up Yap's farm because during such weather he would simply close up the sides on the elevated pens of his laying hens. This farm, belonging to a Mr. Yap, an ethnic Chinese businessman in the Philippines, was on the other side of Tarlac Road. It was heaven to me. Mr. Yap raised white Leghorn laying hens for eggs, but he seemed to like animals in general. So there were dogs with pups, turkeys in pens, a big pond at the front of the property with an island inhabited by monkeys like the one I had kept for a while. They looked like rhesus monkeys, but were smaller.

You could fish in this pond for a fee, and you could rent a canoe outrigger for a fee. Great fun. The monkeys would climb into the boat with you if you went to the island, which of course you were not supposed to do. Now, there was a small stream running from the pond to one at the back of the property. The back pond was off limits because it was the hatchery for the fish in the front pond. But it turned out to be an even better place to fish. So naturally we made that attempt.

All these animals were the most wonderful thing in the world to me. I will never forget Yap's farm. Once a Filipino brought me a crane he had captured in one of the surrounding rice paddies. Not knowing what to do with it, I had it staked by one leg in the side yard. I went off somewhere, and, when I came home, the crane was gone. My backyard neighbors had taken pity on the bird and stolen it out of my yard. They gave it to Mr. Yap. That is how I found out what happened. Well, what can I say. Theirs was the yard all of my chickens used to go into, and nobody remained living there for very long.

The numerous tadpoles I caught were kept in a big metal bowl filled with water – muddy water as time progressed. It was placed on one side of the concrete wash basin where Lori did her work. As the tadpoles began to form hind legs, I put a large rock in the middle of the pan for them to climb out on once their front legs formed, and that is precisely what they did, all at once. Mostly leopard frog polliwogs, they emerged by the dozens – little tender bits of delectable frog.

It did not take the chickens long to figure out what was going on in the backyard. As the tiny frogs advanced across the yard in a mini tidal wave, the chickens, mostly hens, came running up and began gobbling them up. Peck, peck, peck, yummy, yummy, slippery, yummy, peck, peck, peck. Looking to one side from her wash, Lori commented with disgust,

My Early Years in Europe, Africa and Asia

"They make a mess!" Having become absorbed in the massacre, I did not respond.

Most of the events and circumstances narrated up to this point occurred when I was eleven years old, my first year in the Philippines. Somewhere during that period of time I developed a friendship with a boy named Robert. We were good friends. Of course, he moved on base within a few months, and I had to visit him there. His dad was enlisted, so he lived in one of the big, old, white houses provided to the unchristened ranks. These houses were elevated several feet above ground, somewhat like the nipa huts, but not as high, so you could keep things like guinea pigs, etc., under them. You could keep a water buffalo under a nipa hut.

I think I remember Robert having guinea pigs in a pen under the house. I also remember that his dad had a garden in which he grew okra, a rather slimy vegetable that I do not care for. Robert has told me he also gave me one of my ducks. I do not remember that. It rains a lot during the rainy season. Maybe my ducks simply descended like cats and dogs during a monsoon. God knows, it seemed like everything else did.

When Robert and I were twelve, he, his brother, and I were poking around Lily Hill. This is a jungle covered hill situated in the middle of the populated portion of the base. Among other things, there are crashed planes from the second world war scattered through the high grown thickets of trees and brush. There is also a network of tunnels extending under the hill. I do not know if they were once designated for storage or were bomb shelters. They were empty when I ventured into them.

George Lowell Tollefson

The day Robert, his ten-year-old brother, and I were poking around the foot of the hill, we were on a dirt road at the base of it. I believe the provost marshal's office was on the other side of the hill, but we were on the safe side. We were not supposed to be there. At first, we were observing doodlebug depressions in the sand on the road. Sifting through one of these, we began finding old unexpended bullets and started sifting for more. We obtained quite a crop. But in the process we hit something solid. On uncovering it, we discovered that it was the rounded end of a bomb.

The bomb had somehow ended up standing vertically on its fins just under the surface of the road. It sounds incredible, but I later remember an entire Amtrak (an amphibious tracked vehicle the size of a tank) completely buried upside down in the road at the bottom of our hilltop firebase in Vietnam. The heavy rains will do that. There was another boy with us on the Lily Hill road, a couple years older than Robert and I. I do not remember his name. But he was apparently a bit mentally challenged. For he picked up a big rock and dropped it on the bomb. To see if it would go off, I suppose.

Amazed to have survived the experiment, we chewed him out, and he disappeared. We then guarded the road against unwary interlopers and somehow (I do not remember how) notified the ordnance people. When they showed up, the enlisted man in charge chewed us out and sent us away. Not a good idea if one of the boys' mother works in the legal office. She wrote a letter to, I believe, the base commander explaining our boy-scoutish attempts to deal with the matter, and we ended up being commended for our efforts and featured in a

My Early Years in Europe, Africa and Asia

news article, probably in the Stars and Stripes newspaper, a military organ that a combat correspondent friend of mine in Vietnam later used to wrote nonsense for.

This brings up the question of emotion versus reason. Which should be followed, or, if both, in what combination? In our boyish way, we were trying to be reasonable. Of course, the reasonable actions followed a string of unreasonable behavior. We were not supposed to be there in the first place. But never mind that. All of humanity has a problem with balancing the two: emotion and reason. Unfortunately, most of the time emotion takes the upper hand in decision making. At other times, it is the groin that commands, or, at least, it warps reason, emotion, and imagination altogether to its subtle and not so subtle purposes.

The principal cause of this is the work of another powerful element. That is the eternal problem of human egoism, which takes so many forms, but is always present in some form. It can only at best be recognized and controlled but never abolished. It is the primary cause of war and just about every other desperate act. So what to do about it? Well, the record of humanity is basically that nothing can be done about it.

For all our scientific and technological progress, we have not really advanced one iota in the improvement of human behavior. We have become better at hiding some of our more vicious traits, but we have not eradicated any of them. Yet somehow humanity's ascension from the animal world is through the agency of mind. And that means through reason. It is language and its stepchild reason which has raised humanity to its present position. This elevation of the human mind is the case, at least, in reason's own estimate. But perhaps it is no more than an undeserved opinion, the achievements of technology and science notwithstanding.

Reason has provided the gift of time travel. In imagination we can go forward and backward in time, and reason can provide a precise investigation into the meaning of this. That is why we long for immortality. But someday, it is hoped, we will long for decency on a universal scale. Then maybe, just maybe, we will become worthy of our dreams of immortality. Well, enough pontificating. As can be seen, I have a tendency to do this. But should I beg forgiveness for thinking and for hoping that more than a few others might take up the habit? I think not.

The Philippines is a beautiful place, and I do not want to leave behind my best years there, which are my preteen years. But, alas, I must. I got older, hormones kicked in, and I became a human wreck. Already at the age of thirteen I had tried beer at the local sari-sari store and those thin, black, cigar-like Filipino cigarettes as well. Those are the ones Filipino men liked to roll back on their tongues and close their mouths around. Quite impressive to a thirteen-year-old. They blew good smoke rings too. I did master that, but not the former. The problem was that there were no prohibitions against youngsters trying out these things. I never saw any Filipino children do it, nor Japanese children later. But some Americans did, and I was one of them. So ends the age of innocence.

But before I depart from it entirely, I should mention that, as always happened with my overseas American friends, Robert returned to the US after a couple of years. So my next set of friends were a black kid named Fred and his ten-year-old brother. They also were good friends of mine for awhile, but Fred's parents were approaching divorce, and that created problems.

You see, the Air Force had a policy of sending people overseas and not letting their families join them for six months. Well, during that time there was a thriving industry of prostitution in Angeles, and some of the men took advantage of it. Fred's dad was one who did. So, by the time Fred, his brother, and his mother arrived in country, Fred's dad did not want to give up his girlfriend. Hence the problem. At least, that is the way I understood it.

The issue for me was that one day when I came over to Fred's house, he was high on airplane glue and kept inhaling new draughts of it. He wanted me to join him in this. I would not, and after that I never went to see him again. A year or so later, when I encountered him on a bus, he accused me of racism. I did not respond to that, as I often do not respond to various accusations. I am not inventive that way.

George Lowell Tollefson

The Philippines: The Early Teens

The next friend I remember was a young Filipino man named Danny. (Let me point out that I have slightly altered the names of almost everyone I refer to. Exceptions were Lori and Orley. They will always be remembered as being like family to me.) Danny, I believe, was in his early thirties. He lived with his aunt and uncle in a neighborhood on the other side of the road from Balibago, this road being the one leading out from the main gate of Clark Air Base. His uncle, whom I never met, worked on the base, so Danny had access to the base.

Danny apparently also had underworld connections and was an authority in the matter, a boss man. But I did not know this at the time. At any rate, he was a happy-go-lucky guy with a prankish sense of humor. He introduced me to his aunt who served me beer as we sat and talked at her house. I was newly turned fourteen at the time, which for me was an age of great foolishness and little sense. Why Danny took to me I do not know. But he never did me any harm. He was always good natured with me.

Perhaps the most interesting episode involving our association was as follows. One evening he took me to Angeles with him. We rode there in a jeepney. A jeepney resembled a converted, lengthened jeep. Behind the driver's compartment was a covered bed with two long, communal seats, one on each side. Usually as many people as could possibly be loaded into

My Early Years in Europe, Africa and Asia

one of these was. People were picked up and dropped off at various points.

Danny and I went to the red light district. Here we entered a bordello with a hallway and individual rooms on one side at the upstairs level. There was a bench in the hallway, and Danny seated me there and told me to wait. He found a girl and went into one of the rooms. A little later he came out and told me we needed to leave in a hurry. We took off virtually at a run.

It seems the whole idea was that he did not want to pay her for her services. That was his idea of a practical joke. All was accomplished in good humor, at least on his part. I did not observe the young woman's reaction. Danny was fun in that way, always with a smile. Of course, there were those who did not smile, like the cheated prostitute. And, as I said, I did not know of Danny's underworld connections. He never involved me in any of that. He just liked having a rather naive little brother, I suppose.

I learned of his deeper involvements later, when I no longer saw him. Some American teenagers I unfortunately came to know, who were older than me, had a Filipino friend up in Baguio, whom they would occasionally ship things like black market goods and stolen hubcaps to. There was a bus that went from Clark to the American resort in Baguio. It was on this that the goods were shipped – not very many, just enough to make life exciting.

But what I want to say is that when Joe (the Filipino friend in Baguio) would come down to Clark on that bus for a visit, he never left the base. (By the way, most Filipinos have Spanish surnames, but Danny and Joe used American Christian names.) The reason Joe never left the base was that he did not get along with Danny, and he was afraid for his life of Danny and his connections.

My friendship with Danny ended one night after I had made these unpleasant new friends. I got stinking drunk on cheap vodka and ended up passed out in a field not far from my house. Danny happened upon me – or else, given his connections, he knew of my condition. When he found me, he picked me up, took me by the arm over one of his shoulders, and brought me home.

When we arrived, my mother was shocked and ripped into Danny for putting me in that condition. I was in no shape to defend him. So he left under a hail of imprecations, and I never saw him again. Danny was not the type to be seen again, if he did not want to be seen, even if he was in plain sight.

The Philippines was like that then, God love it, full of color and interest. But any misbehavior on my part was my own fault. There were plenty of good people, as well as some bad characters. You chose from the lot. Danny, from my point of view, was a good person, whatever he may have done elsewhere outside my awareness.

But the American friends I chose after him were pretty nasty. I suppose my excuse is that I was young and I was trying to figure out how to be a man. I did not have a father in my life, so I had no models, and I chose bad ones just a little older than myself, but old enough to intimidate and impress me.

My Early Years in Europe, Africa and Asia

I started with Bud, a juvenile delinquent from Dallas, Texas. He was not Hispanic, but he boasted of being a pachuco (a member of a young street gang subculture) and wore a tattoo on his hand which he claimed indicated the same. What did I know? I took his word for it. He was sixteen and I was fourteen. That gave him some authority. He had dropped out of high school in the ninth grade because he could not progress any further. My mother later told me his parents had informed her that he was mentally challenged. But none of this was known to me at the time.

Another "friend" was a seventeen-year-old named Ralph. Bud told me that Ralph was a black belt in karate and nobody would dare mess with him. Probably not true, but close enough to reality to garner my respect. He had a manner about him that did not invite experimentation. The way I got in with these guys was by getting into a fight at school. Bud was there, though I am not sure why, since he did not attend classes.

The kid I fought was big, very big, and Bud encouraged me to take him on. So I did, and he promptly broke my nose and bruised me up a bit. But this proved that I had the moxie, and I was in, unfortunately. This privileged status led to much drinking, heavy smoking, and various episodes of petty theft. For the most part, once or twice, perhaps only once, to prove my manhood, I stole a couple of cartons of cigarettes out of the base exchange. These were no doubt shipped off to Baguio, although we did smuggle such items off base in the Green bus as well. I remember the air police searching the bus at the main gate once. We had the stash under the back seat. I do not know how, but they did not find it.

Such adventures never seemed to quite prove the point. So I was involved in other things, such as climbing over the fence of the base in an off limits area to swim in the river and explore the surrounding jungle country. Ralph claimed to have found a cave with a Japanese helmet in it, perhaps the rest of the soldier who belonged to the helmet as well. I did not witness this, so it remains a plausible mythology. What I do remember is a chicken we bought off some Negritos. It was a scraggly thing, but we managed to butcher it and cook it over an open fire. Not much meat.

Swimming in the river, we encountered a snake floating downstream. According to prevailing expert opinion, it was a cobra. Who knows? The most important thing is that I got caught by the air police on one occasion while scaling the fence. Because I was the one to get into trouble, the provost marshal's office decided that I was the leader of the "gang." I was questioned as to my associates but did not identify or implicate them. This no doubt increased my moxie reputation, a title I did not deserve. How my mother stayed out of trouble over my behavior, I do not know. Perhaps it was her association with the legal office.

At any rate, a worse thing was to come. I believe I was fifteen by this time. I had also dropped out of school, and would later have to repeat the ninth grade, putting me a year behind. But just before the grand event which was to come, someone decided that we ought to have a rumble. Actually, I was still fourteen when this occurred. Supposedly some Filipinos were going to meet us in a big, open field off base. They were the opposition. Apparently, there had been some smaller

My Early Years in Europe, Africa and Asia

fights between Filipino lads and American teens. These had led to the big event.

A number of us were there, strung out in a line, walking across an open field. But fortunately the air police got word of it and were also present in vehicles with bright spotlights. They suddenly turned them on. This broke everything up. To tell the truth, I did not see any opposition, but perhaps they were waiting for us.

We all hightailed it when the spotlights were turned on. I have never been so relieved in my life. Rumbling with rocks, clubs, and perhaps knives was a terrifying thought to me, and I was only dragging myself along because I did not have the courage not to. Had it come to a fight, I doubt my performance would have been impressive. I probably would have simply allowed myself to be beaten to a pulp.

But the real horror occurred later, and I was fortunate not to be along. I am not sure why, other than providence. One night my two principal friends decided that they needed to go into town to get some revenge. So they went with another guy – entirely innocent up to that point – to the red light district in Angeles.

Ralph had broken a wooden stake from a picket fence in what I believe was the second American neighborhood I had lived in: the one closest to the town of Angeles. There was a nail sticking out of the end of the fence stake. They ducked into an alley with this and asked a passing Filipino for a light. He reached into his pocket for a lighter or matches, and Ralph proceeded to beat him with that stake. He drove the nail into the Filipino's head seven times. This resulted in the creation of an international incident. The families of Ralph, Bud, and the unfortunate tagalong were shipped back to the States. The Filipino ended up in the base hospital. I believe he recovered, but in what condition I do not know.

Why, I ask so many years later, would such an incident have occurred? What drives human beings to entertain such hateful enmity over what are largely imagined offenses? Again these are the emotions of animals greatly magnified by an imagination, and, worse yet, a faculty of reason put to the worst possible use. Can we never learn to use reason properly? Granted that reason itself is a limited and faulty instrument, especially when it is invested in things beyond its capabilities. But it is what we have. We ought to discipline ourselves into using it well.

But then, look at me. No human being has ever gone through a slower development than I have. I was in my sixties before my philosophy developed. What was I doing in all that time? For the most part, I was following imagination down blind passageways. I did have some success writing short stories, which I put a lot of careful work into. This certainly required a measure of control. But they did not attract any attention, probably because I did not know how to market them.

Reason is disciplined imagination. It can take a long time both to realize that and to cultivate its use. My short stories were certainly crafted, but they were not all I was capable of, and I believe now that they were not a natural means of expression for me. Art is powerful, though it is by nature indirect. I needed a more direct form of expression.

My Early Years in Europe, Africa and Asia

But often there is not even that level of control. Among a good many people, imagination without reason is likely to get caught up in the physical passions, then magnified by an oversensitive ego. It then becomes an animal with oversized horns, ripping about destructively everywhere. And it is not just individuals, but entire nations, which do this. I would soon learn about the latter case in another Southeast Asian country.

But in the meantime, let me speak of a few more less dramatic things which were observed, heard about, or occurred during my Philippine teens. I should mention the Penitensya, a unique ritual practiced during Holy Week. It is a tradition of self-flagellation practiced in the Philippines in the days leading up to Easter.

People wishing to express self-mortification for the sake of forgiveness of sins and other religious reasons lacerate their backs with whips made of bamboo sticks tied together, and others crawl toward some sanctuary, like a cathedral, bearing a cross. Some penitents are even hung on crosses in order to share in Christ's suffering. The ritual has been practiced for centuries in the Philippines and is only matched in foreigner fascination by the consumption of baluts.

These are fertilized duck eggs that are permitted to develop. Some develop enough to produce an enlarged yolk. But others are allowed to progress to a considerable degree. Then they are hard boiled and consumed as food. I never directly witnessed the practice of Penitensya, but, as for the latter, no thank you. That is a gourmet tradition you have to grow up with to appreciate. I remember being on a cross-country bus once, which

-75-

stopped long enough for half a dozen hawkers of these eggs to shove baskets of them up to the bus windows. Some of the Filipino passengers purchased them with relish and consumed them on the spot, like candy bars. I chose to turn my gaze elsewhere and think of other things.

Perhaps this indicates that I was a finicky teenager. But I did eat dog. That was another delicacy in the Philippines. In fact, I had to be careful no one made off with one of Blackie's pups for that purpose. The dog meat I ate seemed a little tough and greasy. But it may be that it was not properly cooked. I did not continue to experiment in order to discern a difference. I had eaten the stuff on a dare. Always trying to prove something. The only thing I ever proved in those days was the weakness of my own self-possession. Growing up is a pain, especially if you do it at a snail's pace.

While I am on these topics, I should mention that I became intimately familiar with kalesas by means of a motor scooter. A kalesa is a Philippine two-wheeled, horse-drawn carriage that was the predecessor of the jeepney. There were still plenty of them around. My mother purchased the scooter for me when I was fourteen. I immediately sold off all my chickens and bought fuel for the machine, which I used extensively.

One day, zipping a little too fast down a street in Angeles with a friend seated behind me, I turned a corner or came from behind traffic (I do not remember which) and there right in front of me was a kalesa. I had no time to do anything but lay the scooter down on the road. We slid along on the pavement for a considerable distance behind the advancing scooter. Fortunately, we all came to a stop before passing under the carriage. My friend was surprisingly unharmed, but I was scraped raw in several places on my back.

I kept this out of the sight of my mother for as long as I could, but one day she saw the mass of scabs. "What happened to you?" she demanded in surprise. "Oh, nothing." "That does not look like nothing to me!" "Well, I had a little accident." "Little! Your back is covered with scabs." "Is it? I never noticed." "Yes it is. I want to know what happened." My teenage evasiveness having failed me, I gave a full report of the little adventure and received a lecture in return. Since the wounds were healing nicely, I was eventually dismissed with "I do not want to see that again," but my possession of the scooter remained intact.

No, that was not how I lost the scooter. That was the work of my so-called friends. Bud talked me into taking it to a hobby repair shop on the base, and we dismantled it completely. I do not even remember if anything was wrong with it. What I do remember is that that is where it remained – in parts. If it is still there after all these years, it is no doubt of archeological interest.

I mentioned at the beginning of this discourse, or whatever it is, that my mother occasionally had boyfriends. Not often, but now and then. The most memorable of these was a Major Gonzales. He was the chief of police in Angeles at the time, and he would come to our house for a visit armed and with a bodyguard. Needless to say, he did not come to see me. This is the one who would disappear into my mother's bedroom with her, where they "took a nap." As I said, I was fourteen – a little old for fairy tales.

But I never questioned it. I respected my mother's right to what she thought was best for herself. And, to tell the truth, she was planning to marry the old boy, bodyguard and all, the latter generally being positioned outside the gate. I do not mean that it would be a menage a trois. But the bodyguard would have probably long been a feature in their lives. The major must have had enemies.

However, the legal union never came about. One day, during one of his visits, my mother informed him that it was time for him to leave – for good. He protested that he would shoot himself if that was what she wanted. She responded, "Well, you cannot do it in here. It will ruin my rugs." So he departed, body and soul still in complete harmony. Never bluff, I always say. Someone is sure to call it. Then what do you do? You move on.

Now, my mother had a good friend in Angeles besides the major. She was a doctor. They got to be friends through business. The business was the black market selling of groceries and sundry. I went with my mother once when she was making a delivery. I was about fourteen then too – a very instructive year. We climbed a set of wooden stairs inside a wood-paneled entryway. The wood paneling was simply sheets of plywood. We took the groceries to the second floor.

They had been carried through the front gate of the air base in the trunk of our car. The air police never searched her car. After all, she worked in the legal office. And, as she said, some of the colonels were doing the same thing. So why not her? They did not need the money as much as she did. Apparently, one of the things they would do was import a new car with their household goods, then leave it behind when they were transferred somewhere else two years later. Of course, it is best, or at least most profitable, to leave something like that behind on the black market.

The doctor remained my mother's friend, and, when my mother left, the doctor took Blackie to her farm. She later wrote my mother that Blackie would not eat, but would only grieve, and soon died. She even said the dog cried real tears. I still feel bad about it. But I went on to Florida for a few months to a military academy, which did not work out because my mother could not keep supplying them with all the money they demanded in what was literally the company store: school and uniform supplies and the like that I was told I had to have.

Greed! The American god. The true god, I might add. Christianity is largely a front, in spite of contrary claims. This is not to say that there are not some true believers. But I suggest that you could transport them all together to heaven in a teacup and have room to spare for a couple of horses as well.

While I was still in the Philippines, I got to know an American girl I will name Mary. She was like the more famous Mary, sweet to the core. But I did not understand that at the time. This was also when I was fourteen. So when she began to take a serious interest in me, I was hesitant for certain puritanical reasons. She had had a boyfriend whom I knew, and they had apparently been quite intimate. I was still naive enough to want to pick only fresh cherries from the tree of fertility. So I hemmed and hawed a bit. That give Bud time to step in when I was not present. He claimed to her that I had said all kinds of nasty and degrading things about her and

George Lowell Tollefson

certainly did not want her. The reason I know this is because he told me. I never saw Mary again.

My Early Years in Europe, Africa and Asia

Northern Japan

Finally, the narrative shifts to Japan. This is the northern tip of Honshu island, a very cold, windy, snowy place in winter. After the military school fiasco, I joined my mother at Misawa Air Base there. It was a fighter base, but on the large island of Hokkaido north of Honshu a radio listening station also existed as part of Misawa's operations. There was a Soviet Russian presence not far away. Hence the curiosity about what they might be saying. I am sure they were listening in on us too.

Ah, the civility of nations! But since we were both armed with formidable weapons, it is probably best that we each kept our ears to the wall. The Japanese people did not always like this, so there were frequent demonstrations in Tokyo concerning the whole business, not to mention some nuclear weapons which we tried to house in the Tokyo area. Considering Hiroshima and Nagasaki, it is not hard to guess why. Still, Japan should not have attacked Pearl Harbor. That opened the ever beloved pandora's box of retribution.

Today we are King Tut of the world and not always sure what to do about it. Great power means great responsibility and, if history is any lesson, great folly. In many ways the US is still an adolescent, and being a superpower has been a bit of a moral stumbling block for us. We have done good things, but we have also done not so good things. Apparently, it is difficult to tell one from the other. I recommend to the next nation in this position that it bury its head in the sand and totally ignore its vaunted status. It would be better for everyone that way. But there is not much chance this advice will be taken. You have to already be in this position to understand the predicament you are in. And once in such a position, it is hard to give it up. The ego simply will not permit it.

I turned sixteen a few months after my arrival in Japan. As is always the case in regard to military transfers, I was able to make friends quickly. This does not apply in America's small towns. There, where the adults are scrambling to be the big fish in a small pond, the kids form into cliques. It is like one of those bottles some people build model sailing ships inside of. Once in, it is not easy getting out, and, if out, there is no getting in.

Once again we have the human ego at its best. It starts young and never lets up. But when people are constantly transferred to new places via the military, it makes no sense to behave in this manner. If it did, no one would ever make any friends. But that is not to say there are no groupings of common interest. It just means that they are thin walled and can be easily penetrated.

In Japan a major form of transportation and sport is the motorcycle. When I arrived, my mother was a member of a motorcycle club with which she traveled to various places. That came to an end with my presence, not immediately, but shortly after. But, as a result of her having a small motorcycle, she bought me one. Thus all my friends were guys who had

My Early Years in Europe, Africa and Asia

bikes who disappeared during the summer on them. The young resident females did not appreciate this.

There was a teen club, a building usually chaperoned by a volunteer adult. It had a dance floor and, most importantly for the guys, a pool table, which was continually occupied, especially in the winter when the bikes were put in cold storage by base orders and by common necessity.

In that climate in winter, using a two wheeled motorized vehicle was a form of insanity. It was very cold and icy.

In fact, on the road out to my house – I lived off base, of course – which wound through the little town of Misawa, the snow would freeze into impermeable ruts, and the school bus would run off the road into a ditch day after day following the same frozen ruts. One of the things we teenagers did was buy big jugs of Acadama plum wine in the town. I was with some friends carrying one of these when I slipped in the ice and fell into a ditch by the side of the road. I twisted my body and landed on my back so as to save the bottle. But these were not ordinary ditches. They were the sewage conduits for the community. They were open sewers with floating delectables covered only by thin wooden slats.

I do not remember what I did about my unexpected baptism that day. What I do remember happening on another day was walking from my house to a girl's house, which was on the air base. She was the daughter of the colonel who ran the listening ear radio operation up north. On the whole, it seemed that most of the girls had officers for fathers, and most of the boys had enlisted fathers. Presumably, as I was informed much later, when stationed at a Marine Corps air facility in the last

-83-

year of my enlistment, that was because piloting fighter jets restricted reproduction mostly to girls. I do not know if this is true or not. There still should have been an even number of enlisted male and female progeny. But I never took a census.

However, this girl's father was not a pilot. So she was just a throw-in odd statistical factor, as was I. But the point of interest at this moment is the snow. It was a few miles from my house to her house. When I left my house, the weather was clear, and there was no snow on the ground. It started snowing shortly after I left my house. By the time I got to her house, the snow was waist deep on the level. This is not to mention the drifts because the wind was always blowing at Misawa. Blowing hard, hard enough that, when we had to go from the classrooms to the indoor pool at school, the pool being about a block away, we would let the wind carry us along the icy sidewalks. Of course, getting back was a slog, turning sideways, fighting uphill, so to speak.

At such times, the wind would pick up the big metal garbage cans outside the school buildings and toss them around. Winter was parka weather, no doubt about it. There was a permanent ski patrol on base assigned to bring food and necessities to people stranded by the snow drifts. One year a group of teenagers was stranded inside the teen club. But it was not when I was there. Though I do remember the snow piled high above our heads on the sides of the roads.

At one point – I was in the tenth grade – a lieutenant knocked on our classroom door and asked for one of the girls by name. She went out into the hall. There was a moment of silence, then a loud scream. I learned later that her father, a

My Early Years in Europe, Africa and Asia

colonel who was a fighter pilot, encountered a malfunction in his aircraft, so he had to bail out. He did so just off the coast. That meant he was plunged into the icy ocean water. A rescue helicopter was dispatched immediately to pick him up. But quick as it was, it was too late. The man was frozen to death.

I only remember one other plane crash while I was there. I was doing penalty laps around the gym when I heard a loud boom and, looking up, noticed a fireball rising from the runway not far away. There must have been a problem on takeoff or landing, I do not know which.

This reminds me of a civilian airliner crash that took place while we were in the north. My mother was shocked at the number of Americans lost on that plane, so our Japanese housekeeper was comforting her. But there were also Japanese passengers on the plane. I wondered what our housekeeper thought about that. She did not say. At another time, when my mother showed her a photograph of Navaho Indians, she reacted in surprise, remarking that they looked like Japanese.

It is odd how servants are often assumed not to have the same emotions as their employers. And it is even stranger to observe that, when a person is in that position, they often assume a sense of less personal importance. If human beings did not do that, class systems would be much less likely to develop, especially the permanent divisions found in some societies. But the human mind is quite plastic and malleable, which allows for a great deal of exploitation, much of it unconscious at first.

But many times I have observed that working class families will oppress their offspring, not wanting them to get any ideas of being better than themselves. For this reason, Jefferson's ideal of a meritocracy is very difficult to realize. Class divisions readily form and are not so easily dissolved. Democracy in any egalitarian sense is largely an illusion. The ego rules. It either positions itself on top or attaches itself to whomever is already on top. Either way, the practice rapidly assumes a rigidity of form which is hard to break.

The courage to be truly free and independent in spirit is a rare phenomenon, where a person neither desires to dominate nor be dominated. Because of the more common tendency to either grab power or attach oneself to it, every political system, whatever its original constitution, will evolve toward corruption, which is another problem. This is because the great majority of people will continue to take shortcuts of convenience in life wherever possible, including these modes of dominance and attachment, even when they know it will eventually land them and their progeny in unfavorable circumstances. This they prefer not to think about at the time they make their decisions. It is the history of humankind.

I had a number of friends at Misawa, but one particularly close friend was a guy named Ron. But I would drive him nuts. Ron was a very loyal type, who found it hard to brook any disloyalty. Usually at the teen club in winter, when motorbikes were out of consideration, there would be long lines in the afternoon at the pool table. Ron was good at the game. So, once his turn came up, he would hold the table indefinitely, beating challenger after challenger and sending him back to the end of the long line.

My Early Years in Europe, Africa and Asia

There was one exception: me. It was not that I was usually a good pool player. Far from it. But when my turn came up, well, Ron was my friend. So my confidence would rise and peak somewhere in the clouds. I would inevitably beat him because his sense of loyalty would not allow him to play at his best. This happened time and again, sending him to the back of that long line. He would be furious. But he could not change his nature, and neither could I change mine.

Another problem was his younger sister. Naturally, I got to know her, and I decided to date her. He could not handle this because he could not be loyal to his sister and his best friend at the same time. He seemed to think I might do something to compromise her. I had no such thing in mind, but that made no difference. He let me know it was either our friendship or her. I let her go.

Much later (Ron had a bike too) we were in town, and at a crossroad just outside the gate he was hit broadside by a car. It smashed up the bones in his foot, so he lay in the street howling with pain. I ran to the gate to get help, and an ambulance soon arrived, already having been called by the air policemen on duty, who saw what had happened. This incident put him in the hospital and in a cast for a good while. Eventually he accused me of deserting him, and I explained that I had to go for help. So it went, but we were good friends until I left Misawa. I was there a little over a year.

On the whole, there was less interaction between Americans and Japanese than there was with Filipinos. The Japanese were polite, but they kept mostly to themselves socially. We did interact with them in business transactions though. And being not always well behaved teens, we also did some annoying things. One of them involved a local bathhouse for women in the town. We would sneak up and peer through the windows to watch them bathe. They were not overly offended by this, though they did seem a little self-conscious, holding cloths in front of their private parts, etc.

We misbehaved in other ways too. I remember our finding an unoccupied building in town and deciding to make use of it. The problem was that it was full of stacks of paperbound books. So we removed these and rather carelessly tossed them into a back room. The owner was not happy when he found the mess. Apparently, some the books were damaged. He complained to the base authorities and was easily able to identify us on the basis of school photographs. Our parents had to pay out hard cash to compensate for the damage we had done. Probably a little more than that.

This reminds me of a taxicab trip several of us took to get home in a hurry. The cab had a meter, and we ended up touring the entire countryside before reaching our destination. We were not exactly early when we got there. So you see, there were ways of dealing with sometimes bratty American military teenagers. Our parents had to pay for the exorbitant taxi ride too.

Perhaps the most disturbing thing I witnessed in Misawa had to do with race, the usual black and white problem. The most popular guy in our high school was black. He was athletically gifted. Our school was small, so we did not have a football team. But, in great measure due to him, we had an excellent basketball team. He was not tall, but he was fast and agile.

It must be lonely to be a black person at an all white high school. There was only one other black person in the high school, a girl. But apparently they did not see eye to eye, or cheek to cheek, or whatever. Contrarily, the most popular girl in the school was the head of the cheerleaders, not surprisingly, and a white girl.

One evening after dark, someone passed her car outside the teen club, where all the cars and bikes were parked along the curb in front of it, and this person saw the two of them making out inside the car. This was duly reported inside the club, and an atmosphere of scandal was raised. Instantly, these two most popular individuals were ostracized, and they remained that way thereafter. A complete reversal of fortune in the flash of a minute.

Though, of course, I was aware of racial prejudice – snide little observations were everywhere in conversation – I had never witnessed it so pointedly. It truly shocked me, and I have never forgotten it. Nothing else seemed to matter. They had crossed a forbidden line and were immediately erased from the society of their peers. Yet they had been the most eminent members of that society. At least, that is what I thought. Amazing.

I may or may not have mentioned that the principal form of recreation for the group I associated with was motorcycle racing. These were mostly small dirt bikes at Misawa. The base authorities had set aside a hilly piece of countryside on the base for that purpose. GIs as well as teenagers participated in these activities, though the GIs could afford bigger bikes.

There were tracks and hill climbs laid out in a racing course in this place, and scramble races were frequently held there in the summer. My friends and I spent hours out there, when we were not touring the Japanese countryside. For the girls stuck at the teen club, we ceased to exist for months during the day, though we did show up in the evening after dark. Then we were generally clustered around the pool table.

After I left Misawa, two good friends of mine, one having been the only American living next door to me, were involved in an accident on that course. They were there to set things up for the next racing event, and they rode around the track in opposite directions. They could not see each other for the brush along the track, so, coming around a bend, they crashed head-on into each other. I do not know if they were wearing their helmets or not. One of them was not badly hurt, just thoroughly shaken up, but the other guy, the one who had lived next door to me, had his skull crushed. He survived as far as I know, but he was in emergency care for quite some time.

That reminds me of another incident. We sometimes took bike trips to Lake Towada along with some GIs. We traveled there on our bikes and brought along extra clothes and camping supplies in a utility truck (Air Force weapons carrier) supplied by the GIs. It was a big lake, the largest crater lake on the island of Honshu, which is the main island of Japan. Though a fair distance from Misawa, which is on the northern coast with its gray sand beaches and overcast skies, it is still in

My Early Years in Europe, Africa and Asia

the northern part of the island. It is surrounded by forest and is unspeakably beautiful. The color of the water is bright blue because the water is clear and deep, and the surrounding forest is an intense green.

The lake is in the northern part of Towada-Hachimantai National Park. The Japanese definitely know how to designate a park or design a shrine. Towada is both, for there is a shrine on a peninsula which extends into the lake, the lake being nearly round. There are falls, surrounding mountains, forested hills and other attractions. We were there for a peaceful camp-out of a few days. But the event started ominously.

As soon as we arrived, we began unloading gear from the truck and started a campfire. The weather was pleasant, the skies an unclouded blue. However, our trip there had been plagued by rain, and, since we were on motorcycles, we were soaked through. So we changed clothes, which had been packed in duffel bags and suitcases on the truck. Unfortunately, there were also five-gallon cans of gasoline for the bikes on the truck as well, and apparently one of them had leaked onto the luggage.

A red-headed teenager, whom I did not know, put on fresh clothes which were damp with the gasoline and then stepped close to the fire. He became an instant ball of flame. One of the GIs threw him to the ground and covered him with a dry blanket to put out the fire, but he was nevertheless severely scorched with third degree burns all over his body. Much grafting would have to be done, so he was sent back to the States. That was a sobering moment I have not forgotten. We went on to enjoy our stay there, but it was somewhat overshadowed by that event.

At some point, I also attended a cherry blossom festival with my mother and some of her Japanese friends. My mother made friends everywhere, even in Japan in those days not so long after the war. (My age is a precise index of years since the second world war, since I was born eight months after it ended in the Pacific.) I remember the cherry trees full of pink blossoms and crowds of people, but that is all. I tried to look up what I had been told was the name of the place, Sun Dai, but could not find it where I thought it should be. Maybe an old man's memory is a bit befuddled, and this took place later on the island of Kyushu.

Suffice it to say that the Japanese have an exquisite love of beauty. Like the French, they are alive to the senses. But there is a unique philosophical depth of feeling attached to the Japanese aesthetic sensibility. This is not to say the French are not philosophic. Far from it. My reverence for the minds of men like Descartes and Pascal is unlimited. But the Japanese philosophic sensibility is a feeling which is in the soul and ultimately without need of any support from the faculty of reason.

While I am at it, let me momentarily retrace my steps to my tenth year when we lived for a few months outside Tokyo. Behind our apartments, Mount Fuji rose in perfect cone majesty in plain sight. It is not hard to understand why the Japanese revere this volcano, which I assume or hope is extinct. It is majestic and stands there like a monument to Japan, having been reverently painted by such great masters as Hokusai,

My Early Years in Europe, Africa and Asia

1760-1841, and Utagawa Hiroshige, 1797-1858. Such a tendency to revere nature in this way, no doubt a result of both Shinto and Buddhism, humbles any more matter of fact person who is at least remotely capable of refined sensibility.

The Cuban missile crisis occurred while we were still at Misawa, just as the Kennedy assassination took place while we were in southern Japan. In the latter case, I remember Japanese people, strangers I did not know, coming up to me on the street in the city of Fukuoka on Kyushu Island and telling me how sorry they were about the assassination.

In the former case, as teenagers, we became aware of the missile crisis because special ID cards were suddenly handed out to us. These identified us as military dependents, as opposed to military personnel. Supposedly this would guarantee us favorable treatment if we were captured by the Russians. For they were just a quick bomb drop away. Fortunately, the crisis was quickly resolved, and our wallets were simply weighed down with an extra form of identification.

Few people back in the States probably ever think about this. It is not only the service personnel who are on the line overseas. Since they may have their dependents with them, they too can be under threat. But it was not a great source of worry for most of us. Teenage concerns are much more localized.

I remember having a girlfriend, the one whose house I walked to in the snowstorm, who in time became interested in the GIs. In my adolescent jealousy, I was not happy about this and went up to a table once where she was sitting with a couple of them. I told the GIs in a threatening manner that they needed to leave her alone, then walked away. I am sure they were impressed. It is not every day that a thin sixteen-year-old attempts to show off the measure of his testosterone to no avail. What did I think I was going to do? They did not respond.

I am going to insert a few more out of place comments here, not about the above, but in general. I was never much of a reader as a child. I do not think I ever read a single book, but I did read comic books. Did I ever! I would lie in bed with them stacked on the floor and rising higher than the bed. Comic books in those days were thin paper things, and that was a lot of them. But I loved them.

These were not the superhero nonsense of today. For that there was only Superman, Superboy, and Batman. I read some of these, but not often. Rather this was the innocent age of animal characters in comics, such as Donald Duck and nephews, Daffy Duck, Chip and Dale, Mickey Mouse, Bugs Bunny and Elmer Fudd, and so on ad infinitum. I devoured these with relish and did so well into my teens.

It was not until I was in the Marine Corps and would spend my entire paycheck foolishly in a few days, and thus be forced to frequent the base library, that I began to read books. But by the time I got out of the Corps, I was consuming the classics in multiple fields and have never stopped doing so. I am still addicted to that sort of thing, my philosophical interest aggravated by my experience of the Vietnam War.

This reading habit resulted in my reading Che Guevara's rendition of guerrilla strategy just before I went to Vietnam. It was a great help in understanding what was going on there.

My Early Years in Europe, Africa and Asia

Later, somewhere in my twenties, I read Darwin's *The Origin of Species*. This knocked a bit of a hole in my religious beliefs because I was profoundly convinced by the book. It is the only science I have allowed to directly enter into my philosophy without critical evaluation.

Over the following years I tried to reconcile my religious beliefs to it. Naturally I passed up popular ideas such as that all the animals on earth were stuffed into the ark, including dinosaurs, or that dinosaur eggs were included in the collection. But I did try to entertain the illusion that God might have buried fossils and bones in the ground to give the earth an interesting history allowing of systematic interpretation. But eventually I had to let go of that because it seemed dishonest. Why would God stand on his head in order to place our feet firmly on the ground? Nonsense.

Well, my original religious beliefs have steadily eroded since then. By the time my philosophy was formed in my late sixties (that is when I finally grew out of my adolescence), I had conceived of God, or spirit, as universal consciousness with all of phenomenal existence emanating from spirit into human awareness (a limited expression of that universal consciousness) through a condition of mind prior to what we experience as the human mind.

This was the final solution to the problem for me. It did, of course, mean that I would come to suspect the doctrines and stories of Christianity and all other faiths as arbitrary attempts of the human mind to penetrate the ineffable. Underlying these products of pictorial imagination and imaginative reason are genuine intuitions and emotions which act as their basis, and that is why they have endured.

As for myself, my relationship to universal spirit is unchanged from that of my former beliefs. I love God (the spirit), and I have the highest reverence for the teachings of Jesus of Nazareth, insofar as I can determine their original state prior to the considerable amount of embellishment and reinterpretation that followed his crucifixion. But now I will return to my narrative.

My Early Years in Europe, Africa and Asia

Southern Japan

We left Misawa in the late winter or early spring of 1963, not long before my seventeenth birthday. We drove to Tokyo, or almost to Tokyo, in an old Plymouth. Poor thing. I killed it. You see, it was my turn to take over driving late at night because we were doing a straight-through drive. I did well until we were eighty miles north of Tokyo. Then I fell asleep. I remember almost doing so and getting myself out of the oncoming lane just in time. There was that split second of confusion when I wondered why people were driving toward me in my lane. Then, fortunately, I realized that it was not my lane and politely removed myself from it to make room for its rightful owners.

However, this was insufficient rectitude. I soon fell asleep. Crash. I hit a huge concrete telephone pole on the left side of the road. In Japan one drives on the left. The pole did not give an inch. The car did. The left fender crumpled up and was folded into the windshield. I was unconscious, and so was my mother, for she had lain down and was asleep on the front seat next to me. When I awoke, I saw that the car was on fire. Not a good thing. So I woke my mother, and we got out of the car.

At that point a Japanese eighteen-wheeler truck stopped, and the driver hopped out with a fire extinguisher and put out the fire. We stood some distance away. After that, I do not have a clear memory of who did what. But, obviously, someone called an ambulance, which took well over an hour to get to us. It came from Tokyo, which was eighty miles south of us. There was still a little snow on the ground, so we needed a place to stay warm. This was provided by a Japanese family who lived a little ways off the road.

You could not immediately see their house from the road because it was next to some farm fields which were located a considerable drop below the level of the road. But what a beautiful house it was. It was the kind with a bamboo outside veranda and sliding rice-paper walls. Inside in the family room was a large hibachi sunk into the floor with a low table positioned over it. Charcoal coals were burning in it, and they put out considerable heat. We were invited up to the table and sat with the family with our legs under the table and a large, heavy fabric spread over the table, our legs, and waist. There was no central heating in the house, but this kept us plenty warm, and I am sure that my mother provided a sufficient amount of American-style conversation, often loud and slow so it could be understood.

The family was, of course, curious, and we had more than an hour to wait for the ambulance. When it came, we were taken to a hospital in Tokyo, where my mother was x-rayed as a precaution against broken ribs. The reason she was x-rayed was that she told people she was driving, so they thought the steering wheel might have caused some damage. It did not because she was not driving. But, in fact, I was not injured either. My mother always felt guilty about her fib and concerned that I might have had injuries which needed to be detected, but she had to do it because Japanese law did not permit the driving of a car below the age of eighteen.

Well, the car had achieved the status of nonexistence, at least for us because it was totaled. We had to continue our journey to Itazuke Air Base on the southern island of Kyushu by plane. The base is now Fukuoka International and Domestic Airport. But at the time it was a US Air Force facility. It was just outside the city of Fukuoka, where I and my friends spent a lot of time.

The house my mother and I lived in was, as usual, off base. But it was just outside the base, so I could easily drive the car (another one) onto the base, where driving cars was allowed at sixteen years of age. However, motorcycles could be legally operated in Japan at the age of sixteen, and that is what I and my friends used to go into Fukuoka.

Now, this was an interesting house. It was right beside a set of railroad tracks, and every night an express train would roar through, laying on its horn all the way. At first it literally threw me out of bed because I do mean that we were directly beside the tracks. The tracks were elevated above the dirt road that ran in front of the house, and no space was wasted between them. But much more interesting than this from a teenage point of view was the fact that directly next door (within a few feet beside us) was a house of prostitution. The houses and other buildings were built close together.

I remember one night seeing a naked airman standing beside a second story window of that establishment. I did not see his, no doubt temporary, girlfriend. I was disappointed. I casually mentioned the episode to my mother, and she immediately switched bedrooms with me. My friends had fun with that. They were convinced that she did so because she wanted to see the sights for herself. Some of them lived in the same neighborhood, and, when they would come to get me near noon, they would almost always find me in bed with a large stack of comic books, as previously described.

One of those friends was coming to get me on his bike in the same neighborhood when, coming around a corner, he encountered a young Japanese with a pole or bat, which he swung at the friend as he passed. My friend ducked and went on, surviving intact to tell the story in a somewhat excited manner. Our relations with the Japanese were not all like that. I do not know what this one person's grievance was. Perhaps he felt we were making too much noise with our bikes. We did have a habit of removing baffles from our mufflers. It sounded better, we thought. Now I find loud pipes irritating. It is all a matter of perspective.

There was also an incident when a couple of young Japanese men strolled past our house one night in a very inebriated condition. They were making a lot of noise. So my mother went to the door and wanted me to use my male voice to send them away. Instead, I asked if they needed any help, and they said no and quieted down, going on their way.

Like Misawa, Itazuke also had a teen club with appropriate adult chaperones. But there, as at Misawa, it functioned as a rendezvous point for us to do other things, like plan trips into the city of Fukuoka. The city was where we had the bikes repaired, when we needed it. I remember taking my bike in to the mechanic one day to have my clutch fixed. He took so

My Early Years in Europe, Africa and Asia

long, I became impatient, so I started yelling at him. In typical stoical fashion for that part of the world, he acted like he did not hear me, though I was standing right next to him and being quite loud. He did not even flinch. It was truly as if he could not hear me. Maybe he had little valves in his ears which would shut out sound when deemed necessary. Whatever was the case, I made no headway with my temper tantrum. So I learned to wait patiently for the job to be completed, which it was in due course.

The Japanese mechanics I encountered were well trained. There were no novices. They went to schools to learn their trade, and they learned it well. Honda was one of the companies that provided such training. They made the bikes we rode, but they were not yet at the stage of mass marketing cars, insofar as I was aware. However, they were not far from it. They were entering models in car races at the time.

Another place we went was to the rather small food emporiums – that is, little shops which served things like bowls of soba, a buckwheat noodle based soup with other vegetables. We also went to better restaurants. I remember one where we took off our shoes and entered a small, private chamber off a quiet hallway. The tiny room was located behind sliding rice panel doors. The table was low to the floor, and we sat on the floor. We ordered saki and were served it in very small porcelain containers. It was potent, and we thought it okay, but we preferred the usual Akadama plum wine, which was a little like a sweetened port wine, since it is a fortified wine. We ordered it after the sake.

George Lowell Tollefson

During one of our trips into town, I remember a Japanese car turning off the road onto a sidewalk, hitting a medium sized tree planted there, and coming to a stop with the tree lying on top of the car. The driver got out, pushed the tree off the roof of his car, got back in, and proceeded on his way, reentering the traffic in the crowded street. That is how the driving was, different from the US. People did not stick to their lanes, but swerved in and out of the dense traffic, like a swarm of bees. We thought it was great because, of course, this sort of quick in and out maneuvering is what motorcycles do best. And we were reckless teenagers besides.

Every healthy teenager believes he or she is going to live forever. It goes with all those wild, raging hormones. That is what makes setting the military induction age at eighteen so convenient. Much enthusiasm then, generally not much good sense. Of course, it is only the more spirited who succumb to this. The more complacently internally organized follow the properly prescribed routes of education or training, a family, and a career. Not that young enlisted in the military do not get married. Some do, though the military frowns on it, and for good reason. At low rank, the young couples live in poverty at minuscule pay. This was especially true in my time, before the all-volunteer services came into being.

We did motorcycle races in the south as we had done in the north. Motorcycles, or motorbikes if you prefer, since they start out with fifty cubic centimeter engines and work their way up, were very popular in Japan. They were used for sport, and the smaller bikes also provided a cheap and reliable form of transportation.

My Early Years in Europe, Africa and Asia

You would often see some guy on one of the smaller bikes heading down the road with a load of groceries stacked up and tied down on the back. It was the family car for many Japanese. And for good reason. Besides being relatively inexpensive, the bikes were made for those roads. Many of the roads were dirt and deeply rutted, disastrous for cars. The only concern was making sure your kidneys did not bounce out onto the road as you went along from one pothole to another. It is especially difficult to retrieve a lost kidney in heavy traffic.

But then, I am exaggerating. Cities like Fukuoka were also full of small cars. American teenagers on bikes were the exception in the urban setting. And the roads were well paved. It was in the countryside that small motorcycles were popular. In spite of the densely crowded cities, there was a lot of beautiful countryside.

As for the races, some in the south were road races, carried out on a circular, paved track at high speeds. I had a teenage friend who entered a small, but extensively souped-up bike in these races. He had cowlings and a windshield to reduce air resistance. It was quite a rig, and he would go round the track practically laying down on the pavement at the height of the curves. He also wore leathers when he raced. Good idea, considering.

I participated as support in those events. I also served as a spotter in scramble races, along with a number of Japanese. Races were the one place where we mixed together freely. It was a joyous extravaganza – usually. An exception was a Japanese participant I saw go off the track at a relatively high speed where I was acting as a spotter. He went off into rough terrain, wrecked, and was thrown into the brush, where he lay still. I was not the only spotter, and almost instantaneously people arrived to help. The victim was not only unconscious, but apparently his heart had stopped. I saw one of these men pull out a long needle and plunge it into the motorcyclist's chest. I believe he survived. The race went on.

I often mention racing but no other sport, other than a little fishing at inopportune times. The reason is that I did not do well in sports which were centered around a ball. I was in Little League for one season in the Philippines and turned out to be on the winning team. The only problem was that I was the worst player in the league. They would put me in left field, and, when a pop fly would head out that way, I got out of its way. The reason was that I could not look up and gauge where the ball was or where it would come down. So I could not safely catch it. I had a rough time as a result as a star benchwarmer, and I took a lot of verbal abuse and got into fights on account of my being "afraid of the ball."

It was not until I was nineteen and attempting to get into the military that I discovered the cause of my misery. I had no depth perception. At the armed forces testing center they classified me as 4F. I went to see an ophthalmologist, obtained a special prescription with accompanying glasses, and got a waiver from the military. My poor binocular vision (without the glasses) would not keep me from accurately firing a rifle or from getting over and under obstacles, and the military needed warm bodies to fill their body bags. So I got in.

My Early Years in Europe, Africa and Asia

But that was only one of several things that could have kept me out of the folly of the Vietnam War. Nevertheless, in spite of obstacles, I overcame all of them and went, and, in spite of the social negativity which has accompanied my past service all my life, I do not regret the decision. I am proud of the fact that I was not one of those who ducked out of the conflict.

One of my other obstacles was that I had been raised more or less as a baptized Seventh Day Adventist. That made me a registered conscientious objector. Because of this, I was assigned to a supply job and had to work to get out of that. I finally went to a year long language school in Washington, DC, where I spent six hours each weekday learning Vietnamese. North Vietnamese, but close enough. Where I ended up, the language was a dialect somewhere between North and South Vietnamese.

Looking back, I will now grant that the war truly was wrong, and not because we did not succeed in our purpose. It was wrong for reasons of humanity with respect to the Vietnamese people and hubris on our part. Nevertheless, I do not regret going. As a conscientious objector, how could I ignore the fact that, if I did not go because I was morally pure, someone else would have to go in my place? Of course, I did not understand any of the negative arguments in regard to participation at the time.

I should mention the Hakata factory my mother and I went to. She ended up purchasing more than thirty "Hakata Dolls." They were not dolls. They were terracotta figurines, beautifully done, like most Japanese crafts and works of art. They were realistic depictions of Japanese busy at their various traditional occupations, like fishing, fishmongering, a samurai warrior sharpening his sword, a man cutting down a tree, an old couple reading together, etc. Their realism reminds me of Roman busts of known Roman political figures.

These Roman busts are, in my opinion, not sufficiently appreciated as fine works of art, and, it would seem, neither are the Hakatas. The reason for the latter is that they were sold in great quantities to Americans in Japan, and the result was a flooded market in the US, where their market value is not high. Also, not all are of the same quality. But my mother never bought anything but the best, if she could help it, and the ones she purchased were very fine indeed. I remember watching a woman squatting Asian fashion out on the porch of the factory, painting one of these figurines.

I had a girlfriend in southern Japan whom I will call Martie. She told me she was the daughter of a priest, but I did not enquire into it. Her mother had married after that, and her stepfather was in the Air Force. Martie seemed troubled about her origin, but I do not remember such details of it as I might have known at the time. We dated for awhile and considered ourselves "going steady." But one day she was seen kissing another guy, and I was told about it. So we broke up.

I dated a girl of Latin origin after that, who turned out to be quite volatile by my standards. At least, I did not understand the vehemence of her reactions. One day we were at the teen club, sitting on one side of an open room, and an extraordinarily unattractive girl was dancing alone in front of us. She seemed to be quite into it, showing off, and I got the impression that she did not share my view of her attractions. In fact,

My Early Years in Europe, Africa and Asia

she seemed to think I was attracted to her. So did my short-term girlfriend.

At any rate, I found myself staring at her in wonder at her view of herself, and the girl I was dating, who was sitting beside me, became furious with jealousy. She went soaring off into a stratosphere of anger, and that was that, though I have to admit that I never really explained myself. I thought, "How could she think I was interested in that girl?" and left the thought unexpressed. So much for her. I am sure she was happier without me.

Martie and I got back together. This time she promised not to have any side entertainments, and, when I left Japan for the States, we promised to remain true to each other. I wore a bracelet she gave me to that effect. But when I got back to the States, I literally froze with anxiety and doubt as to her sincerity. I could not forget the incident with the guy, and, because of this, I could not write to her. Once again, my prudery had intervened. This went on for weeks, maybe months. She kept writing, wanting to know what was wrong, and I could not bring myself to answer her letters. My mother intervened upon her behalf, but to no avail. Finally my mother asked me to let her send the bracelet back to Martie, and this I did. End of story.

I am a strange duck, I know. Where this prudery came from, I do not know. I think that in some sort of way, I imbibed my mother's disappointments. A landlady had deceived her about her first, and perhaps only, true love by not giving her his letters while he was serving as a Marine in the South Pacific, he being Native American to this woman's disapproval. Then my father had an affair, and that ended their marriage. Finally, my stepfather turned out to be a liar, a thief, and an all-around beast. So that marriage had to end. After that, my mother had little faith in men. So I guess I was having trouble having faith in girlfriends. Of course, Martie had given me some reason. But my behavior was a bit extreme nevertheless. I am sure Martie thought I had found another girl, but that was not the case. My emotions were simply frozen to the point that I could not respond to her letters.

If one could account for all the strange variations in human emotions, the human-molded world would be much easier to live in. The multiple shadings of emotion are a veritable rat's nest of complexity, so most of us end up acting like rats at times. Squeak, squeak. Once again, it is the ego that does this. It throws things out of proportion by centering them on the weakest spot in a person's universe: his or her self. At least, that is generally felt to be the weakest spot, if one is truly honest about it.

But then, honesty with oneself is not a widespread virtue either. Alas, how can you handle a soup too hot to the tongue, if you ignore the use of a spoon to cool some of it off? Self honesty is the spoon designed to get one through life in the heated blend of ego enhanced emotions. Of course, you can always throw out the soup and become a hermit. I have considered that at times in the past – that is, before my present marriage. But I have never had the courage to become what Aristotle referred to as either a beast or a god. At any rate, this sermon aside, I do not think I had the capacity at the time for

My Early Years in Europe, Africa and Asia

the kind of self honesty I am referring to. The emotions were too strong, and my understanding of them nil.

As an aside, I should probably have mentioned earlier that a plain-clothed officer, an Air Force captain, accompanied my mother and me to the airport in Tokyo where we caught our flight to Itazuke. Once we were on the plane, he departed. The reason he came to the airport with us was that there were demonstrations at the time by leftists who opposed the presence of nuclear weapons in Japan. Apparently, the US had some there at the time. Once again, considering the relatively recent experience of Hiroshima and Nagasaki, it is understandable why these demonstrations were taking place. But hell, you cannot play top dog without a big bite, especially when the other would-be top dog is nearby with a similar set of teeth.

George Lowell Tollefson

Stateside

As to why we left southern Japan eight months after we got there, the answer is that my mother developed cancer. We had to return to the States to deal with it. Somehow this allowed her to be transferred to Mountain Home Air Base out in the sagebrush country about forty-five miles east of Boise, Idaho. This is also potato growing country – potato "ranches" no less. But increasing numbers of military people were retiring here for another reason. Mountain Home, though itself in semi-arid sage, sand, and sunbaked stone country, is not far from the forested mountains, where abundant fishing and hunting opportunities are available.

However, we spent at least a full month in Boise dealing with the cancer. It was breast cancer, and it turned out that a radical mastectomy was required. This was at that time – the early nineteen sixties – a crude and dangerous procedure. The surgeons removed not only her breasts but a good deal of the musculature underneath. It left her permanently incapacitated for the rest of her life, and she lived for another thirty-six years to the age of seventy-nine. But, though eventually impoverished, she soldiered on and continued to find meaning in life.

People do that. That is the best part of the human species. We carve a niche for ourselves with whatever tools we can manage. In addition, she had a very strong will. Nothing could keep her down. When she headed into the operating room, I

My Early Years in Europe, Africa and Asia

was there, and, realizing she had only a fifty-fifty chance of surviving the operation, she had called in a relative to take me home with him if she did not make it.

Just before she went in for the procedure, I told her I had prayed for her and had asked for another twenty years and a husband for her. A good one, I meant. She said, "No, no, ask for forty years and no husband." So I did, and she lived for another thirty-six years with no male companion. I guess she had had enough of those and did not want to take any more chances. I cannot blame her. I have been very fortunate with a second marriage, but it did take a second marriage to do it. For the same emotional reasons as stated above, human relationships can be a difficult proposition.

As it turned out, our relative did not need to take me home with him, and we moved on to Mountain Home, a small town about eleven miles from the base and, as I said, forty-five miles east of Boise out in moonland. As always, we could not live on base, but, whereas this turned out to be a blessing overseas, it was a kind of hell in the States. We lived in the town, but I was not accepted because of my connection with the base.

Government contractors had been building what I was told were missile silos there, and this had swelled the town's population to an enormous ten thousand, all with their pockets full of government gold (so I was told). Then for some reason the silos had to be torn out. This resulted in an overnight reduction of the population to five thousand unhappy, impecunious souls. All this I learned second hand, but I do not remember the source.

George Lowell Tollefson

So, as a result of the sudden reduction in prosperity apparently brought on by a governmental decision, the local residents now hated the government and anything connected with it in the usually irrational way most people think. The Air Force is a branch of the government. So they hated it. That means they hated me. Not all of them. I remember a girl my age who helped me with my math. She was in my English class and would walk with me through the halls to our math class. During that walk, she would clearly explain the previous day's lesson. I did reasonably well in that class because of her.

But most of the kids there avoided me enough to render me an outsider, as I have previously mentioned. This reception was quite a shock. I had never experienced it before. Lesson to be learned: never underestimate the human capacity to ostracize, whether in greater or lesser degree. I was not completely cut out, but my friends were not what I had become accustomed to. They were the other outsiders to the community – outsiders for different reasons.

And people want to know why school shootings occur. That is undoubtedly an extreme reaction, but it could be prevented. It is important to recognize that ostracism is a form of bullying. People are social animals, and deliberate exclusion makes some of them behave in unpleasant ways. I just bided my time until I got out of that place. I did so within three days of graduation from high school. I was then on my way to Marine boot training in San Diego. I never looked back.

But I did have a girlfriend from the air base while I was there in the town. She lived on base, a safe distance from the local prejudice. We all – town kids and air base associated kids – went to the same high school, which was in the town. The base kids were bussed back and forth, to and from the school from the base. Later, when this girlfriend got interested in GIs because I did not bother to write, I prospected elsewhere.

For this reason, my mother claimed that I married my first wife on the rebound. Could be. I met her while I was stationed in Washington, DC, attending language school. But who knows? The question is, why did she marry me? Was it because her two roommates had recently gotten married? These are as good explanations as any for both of us. At any rate, the marriage lasted nine years, seven of which we were together, and it did not work out.

George Lowell Tollefson

Marine Training: Boot Camp

I arrived at the San Diego airport with two other new Marine recruits. We were picked up by two Marines in a small truck and hauled out to the recruit depot. We sat behind them. As soon as we were on our way, they started yelling at us: keep our heads straight and our mouths shut. The windows were wide open, so a lot of wind was blowing into our faces. We were unloaded at the depot and assembled with a motley crew of other recruits on some yellow footprints painted on the tarmac in front of the reception building. Standing precisely on those footprints, we were informed that the Marine Corps would be our mother, father, sister, and brother. We were trash, maggots, but they would shape us into Marines. We would not eat, breathe, shit, or do anything else except when told to do so.

This turned out to be true. In spite of the strenuous physical training, I got in the habit of moving my bowels only on Sunday. It was the only time we had to ourselves, though we had to keep our mouths shut, sit on our buckets, and clean our brass, spit shine our shoes, or maintenance our weapons.

The reason Sunday became a day of eliminative rest for me was that it was impossible for me to take care of the matter on any other day. We would be marching or running somewhere in formation, when we would be ordered to stop in front of a building that had twenty-five toilets. Here we were given three

My Early Years in Europe, Africa and Asia

minutes to take care of any business and get back in formation. Urinating was problem enough. Anything else required a time-consuming fistfight. It just was not worth it. Not in three minutes, and this was not a rhetorical command. Three minutes was what we had to get things done and get back in formation. Then we would continue our run or whatever.

When we first checked in at the depot, we were given sea bags (duffle bags) and, after having our heads shaved, we stood in line facing the uniform clothing supply people. Each of us would stand in front of one issuing person, holding his sea bag open in front of him and staring straight ahead. The person issuing whatever – shorts, t-shirt, utility trousers, etc. – would take the item, usually in a plastic bag, and slap it across our face, thus allowing it to fall into the sea bag. We were to remain unflinchingly at attention. Then we would stop neatly at attention in front of the next issuer.

Having completed these welcoming preliminaries, we assembled seventy strong outside to become a training platoon. This is when we met our senior drill instructor in his impeccably neat uniform and Smokey the Bear cap. For some time, I came to regard this man as insane. He was quite temperamental and demanding, the brim of his Smokey the Bear cap on the recruit's nose as he yelled obscenities ornamenting some particular gem of correction for unconscious misbehavior on the part of the individual recruit, such as not making a neat right turn on command. For example, in asking a question, I addressed him as "sergeant" (he was a staff sergeant) and was promptly informed that his name was "sir." "Sir, puke! Don't make that mistake again." I did not.

George Lowell Tollefson

A good deal of the training was physical (aside from mental), and most of the rest of it was drill. Constant marching when not running, sweating, and grunting. We lived in Quonset huts and slept on steel double bunks. We were awakened at five each morning, "Get up, get up, you lazy pukes!" as a large metal GI can was sent careening down the middle aisle between the bunks, crashing loudly into their steel legs. We jumped out of the rack (bunk) in our shorts and landed on our feet at attention, staring straight ahead.

San Diego can be a hot place in the summer. When we did physical training, we laid out our plastic ponchos and did our exercises on them: push-ups, squat thrusts, etc. Pull-ups were another favorite exercise, but, of course, that required a pull-up bar, located elsewhere in the training area. Usually the poncho, when used for the push-ups and squat thrusts, would be covered from end to end in an unbroken pool of sweat.

Our runs were lengthy and generally conducted in thick sand. No doubt that was in part to protect our feet and joints. Concrete and macadam are hard on them. But the immediate effect was to feel as if our lungs were being torn out of our chests. Thick sand is hard to run in, and woe betide anyone who thought to drop out of the running formation. We had a black corporal who often took us on the runs. He was a bit pudgy, but he could run all day, sweat pouring off him.

There was marksmanship training with the M14 rifle for two weeks, but there were no infantry tactics. That would come immediately after the three month boot camp. There, in a similar atmosphere, more physical, but less psychological,

My Early Years in Europe, Africa and Asia

we would receive multiple weapons training and basic infantry tactics.

Reverting back to boot camp before leaving it, I remember one instance when we were doing rope climbing. In this instance, we were ascending a knotted rope. Not too difficult, though we were loaded down with rifle and gear. But there was a recruit in the platoon who appeared to be very slow mentally – perhaps one of McNamara's ideas. He climbed the rope and froze. The senior drill instructor went ballistic when he could not get him to come down. He grabbed the rope, yelling, and began to swing it back and forth. When he did, the recruit just let go and fell to the ground, about twenty feet, landing on his back. I noticed a fine crop of beads of sweat that broke out on the drill instructor's forehead. This could probably have been career ending. But the recruit got up, seemingly unharmed, and training resumed.

Two other things. Shortly after we first began training, we were marching across the large blacktop parade field when we encountered another platoon coming toward us. It was full of busted up people on crutches, bandaged up, and so forth. I thought, "My God, what have I gotten into? The whole platoon?" But this turned out to be the sick bay (medical) detail. These casualties were from multiple platoons, which was a little reassuring when I learned of it.

The other thing was that I was officially a Seventh Day Adventist. The Marine Corps was, of course, not comfortable with that fact, but they made accommodation for me and one other guy in my training series (a series includes multiple platoons). We were allowed to spend an hour with an Adventist minister on Saturdays (the Adventist day of worship). We attended several times, but one day the minister let us know that he could get us out of the Marine Corps. Boot camp was not a pleasant experience. But we took the offer calmly and, upon leaving, the other recruit and I agreed we would never return to that Saturday session with the minister. That was the end of my association with the Adventist church.

My Early Years in Europe, Africa and Asia

Marine Training: Infantry Training Regiment

Infantry Training Regiment (ITR) was different from boot camp, but it was no less rigorous – just in a different way. I should explain that the infantry training regiment was not for people who were actually going into the infantry. It was for everybody else because all Marines are considered to be riflemen, which is the Marine Corps term for infantryman. We were Marines now, so we did not have to call our enlisted trainers sir. But if that implies a more relaxed atmosphere, it was not. I do not think the Corps knows how to relax. What it does do is become more respectful of the individual Marine as he or she progresses in training.

Another thing about the Corps in general is the way it uses language: usually quite crude, but no truth is hidden behind a euphemism. Things are described as what they are in rather ungentlemanly terms. For example, a mattress cover is called a fart sack, and the cloth garrison cap is called a piss cutter. A toilet is a shitter and in Da Nang, Vietnam, there were piss tubes scattered about for convenience. The latter were simply tubes in the ground, so you knew where to aim. You could stop on your way anywhere and empty your bladder in the open air.

All these things had official names, but nobody ever used them. In those days women Marines were called BAMs. That stood for broad-assed Marine. I am sure that term is no longer used. The military is hard to enlighten, but, since Congress pays them, they are capable of learning to mend their ways. My point in mentioning all this is not to show how crude things can be. After all, training to kill people is a bit crude in itself. And that is the point. This language is a reflection of the Marine Corps' peculiar brand of honesty. Hey diddle diddle, straight down the middle. That is the spirit of it in both language and practice. The "straight down the middle" outlook cost the Corps a disproportionately high volume of casualties in Vietnam.

My principal awakening to this ethic came at ITR, when we received gas mask training. We were taken out to a little windowless wooden shack in an empty field. Unlike the more formal Nuclear, Biological, and Chemical Warfare Training Center placard I have since seen outside the Corps, this building had a sign on it that read Gas Chamber. Nothing more. After all, that is how they saw it.

So we filed in with our gas masks on, the door was shut and barred, and we were ordered to take off our masks and sing the Marine Corps Hymn as tear gas filled the room. Naturally, we ended up choking, eyes and lungs burning, and some trainees began to panic. The order was given to get back in line, or we would never get out of there. We were to file out in an orderly manner. The door was unbarred and opened, and we did so. But as soon as any of us hit the doorsill, he took off running out into the field, snot pouring down onto his chest. End of gas mask training. I am not sure how effective it was. I personally

My Early Years in Europe, Africa and Asia

was always terrified of gas masks after that because I thought any such repeated training would be the same.

Now, we did learn a lot during ITR (Infantry Training Regiment) training. Much ado about various weapons and the like. Important things, such as putting one foot back to brace yourself when you ignite the flame thrower. The fuel mixture is thick and heavy and is forcefully ejected, and, if you are not properly braced, its sudden pressure will result in you falling backwards, shooting the burning material straight up over your head. When it comes back down, you can kiss this life good-bye.

I am glad I never had to use a flame thrower in Vietnam because I probably would have forgotten that rule. In fact, I never fired any weapon at the enemy, though I did serve under fire. The reason for my negligence was that, as an interpreter, I normally carried a forty-five caliber pistol, designed for very short range. So I would help run ammo up to the line when the stuff hit the fan and do things like that. Significant exposure, but greater usefulness. When going out from our firebase to line units, I did sometimes carry an M16 rifle, but I seemed to always come under fire when I had the pistol. The pistol made me look like an officer, so that invited sniper fire too.

As for ITR, we did a lot in the way of basic tactics. Very basic. We had Combat Town and barbed wire entanglements to crawl under while a machine gun fired steadily just over the wire. Quite realistic, but not tactics as such. Just how to keep your head down. But this is pretty much what I mean by tactics in relation to ITR. As for keeping the head down, this was reinforced by the "troop leaders."

George Lowell Tollefson

These were our trainers. They were short-timer veterans near the end of their enlistments and waiting to be discharged. They were tough and a little light on sympathy. I remember the attitude when I came back from the war. It was: "What can they do to me now? I have already been to Vietnam. So I do not really care." When we were learning to crawl in the mud, we were ordered to keep our heads down and dig a groove in the ground. If someone lifted his head, a troop leader would stomp on his helmet, yelling about digging a groove.

Later, when we were running a short course by throwing ourselves behind a log, firing a blank practice shot, and then sprinting to a hole beyond for cover, the guy ahead of me did not do it right. I think he forgot to do his practice shot. A troop leader observer ran over and kicked him in the mouth. So, when it was my turn, you can bet I did it right. I needed my teeth for chewing the slop in the mess hall.

We did a lot of running, just like boot camp. There was a tall, steep hill behind our huts called "Old Smokey." One day a recruit got a package of cookies in the mail. He was ordered to soak it in a bucket, then eat it, after which he had to run up that hill. Another disciplinary act was to have a recruit hang from his wall locker by his elbows for awhile. He was ordered to talk to the little green man. Life was always interesting in this way, but, strangely enough, we grew ever more loyal to the Corps.

We only got two weekends off during this month of training. But that was a very nice thing after never having any free time in boot camp. Before we left on those two weekends though, we had to settle our differences. We gathered in a

My Early Years in Europe, Africa and Asia

circle, and the grievants were installed in the center, outfitted with boxing gloves. They went at it while everyone yelled for or against each pugilant fighter. After that, we got haircuts and left for the weekend, spent either in Los Angeles or at one of the nearby beaches. We usually did not do much. Just wandered around. But the freedom was priceless.

One time while at ITR, we were being heavily exercised as punishment. We were in the field for a few days, and I and two other guys had neglected to shave. Naturally this was observed by the trainers, so, after the entire company was subjected to a couple of hours of push-ups, sit-ups, squat thrusts, etc., the three of us culprits were stood up on a picnic table in the vicinity. The trainers liked to bellow our instructions from these tables. This time, they pointed out to the whole company that we were responsible for their misery. Then they asked what they should do with us. There was a pause and complete silence. Then with one voice the troops shouted back, "Let them go." So they did, and that was the day I truly became a Marine in the depths of my being.

Combat Town was not really a town. It was a small building with a stairwell inside. We entered and ascended to a landing. At that point the stairwell continued on upward from the landing to the roof. But it also turned a hundred and eighty degrees and descended toward the ground floor. When we reached the landing, we were supposed to yell "fire in the hole" and toss a practice grenade into the descending stairwell. The guy in front of me did not remember to do that in the excitement and rush of the training. So he was thrown part way down the stairwell by the enraged observing trainer.

George Lowell Tollefson

On the roof we were supposed to extend one leg and the arm holding a rifle over the eave, then drop to the ground below. Again the guy in front of me did not do it right in the rush and was shoved unceremoniously off the roof. Neither of these two were injured, but I was duly impressed and did my best to remember what I was supposed to do and how to do it correctly. That was Combat Town. Not much to it.

Live grenade practice was different for me. I was unduly nervous for some reason. Fragmentation grenades are rather nasty, you know, if they go off in the wrong place at the wrong time. I was overly aware of that. So, when it was my turn inside the little concrete revetment with a trainer, I did poorly. My job was to toss a few preliminary practice grenades outside the hole. I think I did three of them, and they all bounced off the side of the revetment, joining us inside. The trainer in a weary voice finally said, "Throw the live one now, and get it right." Then he squeezed himself as tight as he could into an opposite corner of the square and very small revetment. I threw the grenade, and it sailed neatly over the hole and landed some distance away, where it exploded conveniently. I have got to say, that trainer had guts. I am glad I never got that job.

My Early Years in Europe, Africa and Asia

Supply School and Barstow

My next port of call was supply school at Camp Lejeune, North Carolina. This, to say the least, was not what I wanted. I joined the Marines to go to Vietnam, but knowing little, I went in on an open contract. That meant they could put me anywhere. So they stuck me in what was intended to be an administrative desk job: a good place for a questionable possible conscientious objector, should I have a change of heart. Even if I ever did get to Vietnam, I would likely be stuck in the rear somewhere, insofar as there was a rear.

There were only a few places in South Vietnam that were not subject to attack. However, the number of instances of enemy contact could be fewer on some of the larger bases and might be subject to only an occasional rocket attack. I wanted to *experience* the war. That meant coming into contact with local villagers as well as the Viet Cong and the NVA (North Vietnamese Army). I had entered the Corps at the end of May, 1965. There were no protests against the war that I knew of, so I had encountered no objections to the sensible nature of my actions.

Supply school lasted six weeks and was sufficiently dull. The only memorable thing that occurred is that I inadvertently got into my first and only barroom brawl. It was a somewhat lugubrious affair. A so-called friend of mine – call him a casual acquaintance – had had a little too much to drink, and when we walked into a place called Birdland, or something like that, in Jacksonville, North Carolina, he picked up a chair and hit a guy with it.

The place had a band, served lots of beer, and was packed with Marines. They all rose to their feet at once and proceeded to swing fists, chairs, and beer mugs. My personal contact was with a beer mug, I believe, on the back of the head, and I hit the floor. There I was kicked in the face a few times, turned my face inside my arms, and passed out.

When I awoke, still on the floor, all was eerily silent. MPs (military police) were in the room, all the other brawlers were lined up, the police were standing outside the door (they apparently preferred to let the MPs do the grunt work), and the band was standing demurely out of the way. I got up and started turning chairs over, not realizing that I was bleeding profusely from the back of my head.

So I was taken on base to see the corpsmen, and the rest were booked for a court appearance. The corpsmen sewed me up without Novocaine, since, as the sewist told another corpsman, I was a tough Marine and did not need any. Because of that court appearance, the few booked people who were in my class missed a day's instruction, and I did not. These were my closest competitors. So the result was that I got the highest score on the final test, and that gave me the highest score in the class. Consequently, I was promoted to the next rank: private first class.

That was supply school. My first duty station was Barstow Supply Depot in southern California. There I reviewed computer punch cards in search of priority 02 items destined to be

My Early Years in Europe, Africa and Asia

sent to Vietnam. I had quit smoking in boot camp, but now I had to start up again to stay awake. I did that and did my job willingly, accepting a late shift without complaint or attitude, and that resulted in another promotion to lance corporal. But I got out of that place as soon as I could. Within six months I was on my way to language school in Washington, DC, to study Vietnamese. Another school was the only way out of supply.

I should mention that when I first arrived at Barstow, I was required to spend a month out in the desert practicing infantry tactics. At one point, we were to take a hill, and, marching out to it, I lost my blanket roll off my pack without noticing it. Someone did pick it up, but they did not return it until after that night. We bedded down on the side of a hill, and, without blankets, it turned out to be one of the coldest nights I have experienced. Deserts do that. It had been hot during the day. This was the Mojave Desert. Darn few plants. I wrapped myself around a tiny, naked bush for warmth and received none. But that was all there was.

So, as it turned out, I only did supply administrative work for five months, since the first month was grunt month. I believe my commanding colonel helped me get out of there on the language school ticket. I was not told this, but he was the one who gave me the meritorious promotion, and he had asked me about my ambitions in the Corps when he gave me a ride to work one day. When the time came, and I had passed the proper test, I was practically led by the elbow through the checking out process.

George Lowell Tollefson

Language School

In Washington, DC, I was quartered at the Naval barracks in Anacostia. It was a poor neighborhood, but the barracks, of course, was on a military reservation. My classes were downtown. Six of us, I believe, attended that class in uniform. We were the student body and were all enlisted Marines. The Marine officer students were in a room next door. We spent six hours a day five days a week in class for forty-seven weeks. At the end of that training period we were certified interpreter/translators.

However, our instructor was a North Vietnamese refugee. She and her husband had left Vietnam in 1954 at the time of the partition. They were part of the migration of a large number of Catholics out of the north. The two of them ended up in the States. Her husband worked for Radio Free Asia. We had workbooks, and we followed these, the instructor providing pronunciation and information on the various accents of a tonal language. What she could not supply was any explanation of grammar. So that we never learned, and it adversely affected my confidence with the language, though I did manage to do my job when required.

At any rate, Washington had lots of night clubs and drinking establishments. It was not conducive to scholarly habits, which I knew nothing about at that time. I had been promoted to corporal upon my arrival in Washington because our com-

My Early Years in Europe, Africa and Asia

manding officer there wanted an NCO (noncommissioned officer) for what was then the seven Marines in the barracks. Another person was also promoted in the same way. But he stuck pretty much to himself. I was a little too well acquainted with my fellow Marines, and that led to my getting into trouble.

We had been ordered not to live in town. Several guys did rent an apartment, and I was there one night when they had a party. The next morning another guy and I were hauling a bed sheet full of beer cans down the stairs, laughing at the trouble we were having with the load, when we looked up and there was the Top (our first sergeant) standing at the base of the stairs. I was the NCO, so I received nonjudicial punishment. I was fined, restricted to barracks (other than class) for two weeks, and given a suspended bust. That meant I did not lose my rank, but it went on my record.

The Marine Corps is very good about noticing the positive things you do. You do not get lost in the crowd. But it has a memory like an elephant. That is because the proceedings were set down in my record book. And these record books are duly read by those in authority who matter wherever you go. So it was two and a half years before I was promoted to sergeant. That was the price of my immaturity. And it did affect my future in other ways because, just before the incident, I had decided that at the rate I was progressing I would make staff sergeant before my enlistment ended. If I did, I decided that I had too much invested to get out, so I would reenlist. But if I did not make staff sergeant, I would get out. I made sergeant, but I did not make staff sergeant.

George Lowell Tollefson

Hence my future as a writer and philosopher was assured, but not until after numerous decades of struggle. Do not become a writer, if you can help it. It must be an incontrovertible addiction to provide the grit to stay with it, unless you hit upon something easy, popular, and ultimately worthless. That was not likely to happen to me. I am a rather contrary fellow.

Hell, my decades long adolescence alone is an indication of my uniqueness. What normal person would take so long to reach a goal he did not fully comprehend for six decades? My excuse is that the philosophical system developing in my mind required lots of time for a largely unconscious, or semiconscious, gestation. I thought about its various components at times, but they did not suddenly come together until I was teaching philosophy. Then it was all there, and I suddenly knew it was.

Why so long? I do not know. A good philosophy is complex, touching points not usually thought about, and mine certainly is that. But many thinkers have gotten where they were going when they were relatively young. Perhaps it was that I long thought of myself as a short story writer, in spite of obtaining a graduate degree in philosophy by the age of thirty-seven. But it is never easy to understand oneself, or anyone else for that matter. And so much of what grew into a system in my mind did so without much notice on my part. I would think about various philosophical problems at times, but I did not integrate them into a complete system, until suddenly there it was.

That was, as I mentioned earlier, when I was in my early sixties. Following that, I quit teaching after five and a half years and spent ten years writing the three central texts of my system. Now I am simply waiting for old age to finish me off. But I am still writing, as you can see, just not on the level of those books. My wife is a writer too of carefully researched historical novels set in old New Mexico during the Mexican and early American period. They are very good, and we enjoy being together. It is the simple things in life that matter. You may have to be old to fully realize that.

George Lowell Tollefson

Vietnam: Division and Regiment

I arrived in Vietnam at the age of twenty-one. This was July 1967, and the first thing you notice when getting off the plane is the hot soup you plunge into. The air is stifling if you are not used to it. But like all things, you do get used to it, more or less. Besides, the climate in Vietnam is a lot like that of the Philippines. So is the vegetation. Home sweet home. A lot of Americans did not think so. During their Vietnam tour, the United States was referred to as "the world." That is how alien this tropical, warring country seemed to most American GIs. Even for me.

In the Philippines war was everywhere. But it was history. In Vietnam it was history being made, and none of us knew how it would turn out. We assumed the fight against communism was necessary and we would prevail in the end. We certainly had the technology and firepower. And, contrary to what some World War II and Korean veterans thought, we did our job and did it well. But what we did not know is that we were there on a foundation of suppositions and falsehoods. We also did not understand how much the Vietnamese would be willing to suffer in order to prevail.

Vietnam became the first war America lost. But I feel no shame in it. We were asked to do what could not be done: fight an enemy with sanctuaries outside our reach and, quite honestly, with right on their side. We were propping up a corrupt government in Saigon, but those of us who were peons in the field were not aware of that either. The US still tries to do nation building with equal unsuccess. It is an expression of national vanity, not national purpose. We need to improve our republic from within and let others construct their societies in their own way.

But enough of this crying in one's beer suds. I arrived at First Marine Division Headquarters in Da Nang, and I and a number of other members of translator/interpreter teams spent three days there while a decision was made as to what to do with us. The decision was to break up the teams and farm us out individually to units in the field. We were like surplus ammunition from a previous war. We needed to be expended somewhere.

I was sent to the Seventh Regiment of the division. That meant bidding a jovial farewell to the field of piss tubes. There were fewer on the firebases, so I never saw so many of them in one place again, except when I came in to Division once a month to be paid. I had to do this because I was administratively attached to Division Headquarters, though I was operationally attached elsewhere.

It was an interesting arrangement, used extensively in Vietnam. Companies, battalions, even regiments were often separated from their parent units and temporarily assigned to others. All this took place in I Corps, the section of South Vietnam where two Marine divisions were assigned, the First and the Third. Towards the end of my tour of duty, several Army units were moved into I Corps. This resulted from the

George Lowell Tollefson

Tet Offensive, which occurred in the middle of my tour. After that, I was gone and did not look back, until now.

The Seventh Regiment's command post was located on a hill, Hill 55. The fifty-five designates the elevation of the hill in meters. As it turned out, the Corps was quite fond of hilltops, for obvious reasons. It is better to shoot downhill than uphill. Because of the angle of fire, the person shooting downward engages a broad range of targets, whereas a person slogging and shooting uphill has a very narrow target range and is very much exposed to enemy fire from above.

When I arrived at the regimental CP (command post), a USO show had just arrived by helicopter. There were four performers, and they were quite nervous because a lot of shooting and detonation of grenades was taking place in the jungle on one side of the hill. The performers did their act on a simple wooden stage hastily built for that purpose. In spite of the firefight and the continual rattle of automatic weapons and shouts, there was considerable attendance at the show, for the Marines were sitting on top of tanks and amphibious vehicles parked in a ring that encircled the stage. They were outfitted in helmets and flack jackets. Most had M16 rifles. Some had M60 machine guns and grenade launchers, and the machine gunners were covered with belts of ammunition slung over their chests and shoulders. They were quite intent upon the show and oblivious to what their fellow Marines were doing a few yards away. Well, they could not be seen anyway. The brush was too thick. But this did not ease the minds of the performers. I do not think they were expecting to be that close

My Early Years in Europe, Africa and Asia

to the shooting war. Eventually a chopper arrived and took our guests away.

I was new and knew nothing. So I had to learn about the war the way every newbie does, by making mistakes. Almost as soon as I had arrived, I was ordered to proceed to one of the two checkpoints at either end of the hill on a dirt road that ran through the CP. At that checkpoint I met a lance corporal on guard. Standing near him was an old woman carrying a heavy load of straw baskets slung from either end of a bamboo pole. I do not know what was in the baskets, but I soon learned they were very heavy.

The woman was old, bent over, and wrinkled, not my vision of someone who would be carrying so much stuff. But, of course, she was a Vietnamese peasant, and these are a tough, wiry people. The woman said she wanted to pass through the compound on her way to market. The guard was waiting for a decision to be made by a greater authority. I outranked him, so, in my total inexperience, I made that decision.

I said I would take her on through, which I did. I also, rather naively, took charge of the bamboo pole with its heavy load of baskets. I was surprised at its weight as the sharp edges of the split pole cut into my shoulder. As we trudged along through the compound, several Marines looked at me in wonder. Why is the fool carrying that pole? they no doubt thought. But what was far more important, though it did not register with me at the time, was that the old woman was looking around surveying everything. Did I ever play into that deception!

A few days later, we received a complimentary call after dark. We were attacked, and a sapper unit made it through the wire. They killed six of us and wounded twelve before they could be effectively dealt with. Though the entire perimeter received fire, I was not at the point where the breach was made, but I did soon learn that they had managed to place satchel charges and explosives everywhere.

I was only with the regiment for two weeks before I moved on to its Third Battalion about two miles down the road. But in the ensuing months some of the undiscovered explosives that had been planted by the sappers detonated, and several Marines were wounded. I knew one guy, an Alaskan Indian, whose hand – I forget which – was badly scarred from the event. He was at a listening or observation post outside the perimeter when it happened. Later he transferred to one of the Third Battalion's line units, which is how I came to know of it.

My next assignment was to question a bunch of detainees who were temporarily quartered on Hill 55 in a big tent. These detainees had been rounded up from the villagers associated with the Viet Cong who had been in the firefight at the time of the USO show. It was a village you could not see because of the thick brush jungle growing on the side of the hill outside the compound. This village was always a problem and was eventually destroyed.

I remember passing the hill months later and noting that the village and jungle had been razed. I asked the person I was with what had happened, and he said the village had been destroyed by a flamethrower tank. Maybe. I do not know. I do not recall any blackened area. So it might have been defoliation. But I do not know if such a small, targeted area would have been dealt with in that way. At any rate, the village was

My Early Years in Europe, Africa and Asia

gone and depopulated, either as permanent detainees or relocated somewhere. But, given all the trouble associated with them, I am betting that they were permanent detainees. Where would you want to relocate them?

The day I did the questioning, I encountered two sharp-tongued young women who knew just enough English to call me a "fucking Yankee imperialist" and other pleasant little sobriquets. They were very young, probably about sixteen, and were most likely Viet Cong nurses. I basically ignored them, though I probably should not have done that either. This is the way you learn in such situations: on the job training. I was destined to learn fast.

I also remember meeting a guy at the regimental CP who had been in the firefight at the time of the USO show. Several of us were standing by a water buffalo getting a drink. A water buffalo is a big tank full of clean water which is hauled into the field by a truck. What the guy had to say was that he had undergone a near miss. He opened his flack jacket – which had individual hard plates inside it in those days – and showed where a bullet had gone inside the jacket, skimmed all the way around it on the plates and exited it on the other side. He was untouched. A near miss indeed. And a rather freak occurrence.

That reminds me of a time at Infantry Training Regiment where we were shooting at moving targets. The targets were held in the air by Marines down in a narrow concrete revetment. I was in one with another guy, and we were walking back and forth holding the targets that other people were firing at, when a stray round zinged into the revetment with us. It ricocheted around, hitting the sides of the revetment as it went, until it grew tired of its labor and came to rest in the lap of the other guy. I think it was the other guy and not me, but I do not clearly remember. The bullet was still warm from bouncing repeatedly off concrete, but it was clearly exhausted. I would be too, if I had to go that route. I am glad it was not interested in passing through one of us.

There was one other incident I recall at the regiment. It involved a badly wounded girl. She had a nasty hole in her back, a shrapnel wound, and had apparently run away from the civilian hospital in Da Nang. A Marine patrol picked her up and brought her to the regimental CP. It was only later that I became acquainted with the hospital and understood why she ran away. I tried to calm her by telling her not to worry, but that was hardly comforting. A South Vietnamese interpreter came up and was able to calm her. I do not remember what he told her. Maybe he assured her we would not return her to the hospital. But we probably did. What else could we have done with her?

My Early Years in Europe, Africa and Asia

Vietnam: The Battalion

As I may have previously mentioned, my lack of grammar, and probably extensive vocabulary as well, precluded me from being able to translate captured documents. So I was sent on down to the battalion. There the commanding officer of the battalion ordered that I should attend medcaps in the morning to give me a chance to improve my Vietnamese. A medcap is a temporary field clinic that provides limited medical care to local populations. It is usually conducted by enlisted Navy corpsmen, sometimes, but rarely, by a doctor. I went along to interpret and provide security.

I should mention that enough years have passed that I can no longer remember the sequence of events I wish to relate. So I will have to randomly describe them as they come to mind. I have pretty much been doing that anyway. Now it will be all the more the case.

To get to the battalion command post from the regimental command post was a two mile trip along a dirt road. Every night the Viet Cong would plant land mines in the road, and every morning, before traffic could pass down it, the mine sweep teams would clear the road, starting from either end and meeting in the middle. The road was known as Liberty Road. But later, after I had returned to the States, I was told that the road eventually became known as Ambush Road. That was a good name for it. Ambushes on it were frequent.

George Lowell Tollefson

The countryside lining the road on either side was made up of rice paddies and impenetrable brush jungle. It was incredibly, intoxicatingly green – very beautiful, if only you could enjoy it without having to be on the lookout for trouble. These brush jungle tree lines were along the edges of the rice fields and were a good place for snipers and bushwhackers to hide.

I myself was caught in one of those ambushing episodes. Having had to go into Division at Da Nang on my monthly excursion to get paid, I was returning in a utility truck, the bed of which was loaded with crates of ammunition. I and several guys returning to our line units were sitting on the crates of ammunition when suddenly the shooting started. They were shooting low, and we could hear the bullets hitting the wheels of the truck. But we could not see anything in the dense brush of the tree lines. So we, meaning the guys with me who had M16s, started firing randomly at the trees. The driver stepped heavily on the gas, and we careened onward to the battalion CP.

When we got there, we hopped down out of the truck. As I walked away, I noticed Marines gathering around the truck, so I looked back. It was then that I saw that there were creases on the rims of the wheels and one of the tires had been flattened. I could not help reflecting that if our bushwhackers had aimed a little higher, putting some rounds into the bed of the truck, they would have hit the cases of ammo we were sitting on and would have blown us to bits. So a flattened tire did not seem like much of a loss.

There was a similar incident later when the driver of a truck was shot in the neck. He did the same thing. He leaned on the

My Early Years in Europe, Africa and Asia

gas and got the truck safely to the compound, where he died from the wound. Because of these incidents, there was a policy of alternately declaring the road a free fire zone and a controlled fire zone. It was normally supposed to be a controlled fire zone, meaning you could only shoot when shot at. This "controlled" designation was to prevent trigger happy Marines from shooting up the countryside. But when an ambush occurred, the road became a free fire zone for awhile.

The battalion commander established these conditions. When the condition was free fire, anyone was free to shoot at whatever to his heart's content. This meant all eyes were on those paddies and tree lines. Anything suspicious was engaged. We were also supposed to travel in convoys during such times for added security. But this was not always possible.

For example, when I and the S5 (civil affairs) lieutenant would have to go into Da Nang for some reason, say to the civilian hospital, we were not in a convoy, regardless of the current status of the road. At such times, I usually traded weapons with the other enlisted person I worked with and carried his M16. Never once, when I had the M16, did I ever come under fire. I always had the forty-five caliber pistol when that happened. That pistol fit so loosely in my holster I would jam my combat knife with its scabbard behind the holster to tighten the holster so the pistol would not fall out of it.

Once, I went down that road with a South Vietnamese Army soldier. I had been ordered by the colonel to do so because the soldier's unit needed timber to build bunkers. So we went into Da Nang to find some wood. We switched hats. I wore his beret, and he wore my soft cover (a cap). It was in the morning. So we passed the mine sweep patrol working their way down the road from the battalion CP end. That meant for a while we were in a situation where we could hit a mine.

So, typical of troops in Vietnam, the ARVN (Army of the Republic of Vietnam) soldier, who was driving, hit the gas peddle, and we flew down the road. This idiotic maneuver, practiced by nearly everyone, was supposed to position us on the other side of the mine by the time it went off. Ridiculous idea. But it felt reasonable when it was the only option. Eventually we passed the other sweep team coming from the regimental CP. They looked at us, particularly me, like we were crazy.

We went on to the Navy shipyard in Da Nang, but could find very little good wood. So heading back, we passed a lone Marine guard at an outpost marking the outskirts of Division Headquarters' area of interest. Not far from him was a nice pile of lumber. He explained that some Air Force guys were planning to build a small building there. We told him what we needed it for. So he looked the other direction while we piled it into the truck and took off. I wonder what became of that guard.

We were about halfway back when we stopped for a bowl of soup in a village. Then, as the sun was going down, my erstwhile temporary friend became concerned that he would not get back to his unit before dark. He wanted to leave me in that village to hitch a ride with any American vehicle that might come along. There was no way I was going to be left alone in that village. He seemed to know those people, but I

My Early Years in Europe, Africa and Asia

could imagine Viet Cong coming out of the woodwork as soon as he left, or after dark when I would be stuck there for the night.

So we argued, him sitting in the driver's seat, and me standing on the road inside the door on the passenger's side. As we argued, my right hand slipped down to the pistol grip on my forty-five. I hardly knew I was doing this, but I was not going to be left behind, one way or another. He noticed it, and the argument ended. He took me back to my unit, then proceeded on to his. The one thing I feared most in Vietnam was becoming a prisoner of war. The war could drag on forever, and I could be a prisoner forever. No way, if I could help it.

The day we (the ammo truck with Marines in the bed of it) entered the battalion CP compound a little shot up and I turned back to see the damage to the wheels of the truck, I noticed some village women inside the compound squatting in a circle, some of them keening. I wondered what they were up to, so I wandered over to have a look. They had some baskets with them which they had set upon the ground. Inside the baskets, the contents were covered with banana leaves. As I walked up, one of the women pulled the leaves aside in one of the baskets. There was a small child, an infant, there with the top of his or her head missing. The blood was dried and purple looking along the jagged edges of the skull. There was nothing inside the skull.

I do not know what happened, but this sort of thing was not uncommon. Perhaps a stray mortar landed near the child. Or an artillery round. Civilian casualties of this kind occurred in various ways. A child might be playing with an undetonated mortar and have it go off. These people were living and farming in the middle of a battlefield. They had no way of avoiding it. They just lived with it, quite calmly, in fact, to all outward appearances.

You would see villagers along the sides of the road with their produce spread out: a minimarket. They would be talking, chewing beetle nut, laughing. Then a tank would come along, loaded with infantry on top – in a hurry to get somewhere. The people would scatter off the road, and the tank would roar past, oblivious to anything but getting where it was going. After it passed, the people would gather back in their original place, and the market haggling would go on.

People working out in the rice paddies never knew when they might find themselves caught between warring factions. Say an American patrol comes along, and it is fired upon from the further tree line. All hell breaks loose. Bullets flying everywhere. The Americans would not by any means be out to harm the unarmed farmers, but neither were they going to overlook being fired upon. So possibly more casualties.

Also, there was of course the suspicion that these villagers must have known the Viet Cong were waiting nearby in ambush. How could they not know it? On the other hand, what would you do if you were such a villager? To tell the Americans that danger lurked nearby was certain death for the informant. A Viet Cong contingent would arrive in his village in the middle of the night, drag him out of his hut into the village street and put a bullet in his brain.

We had something like that happen at the battalion CP. There was an old guy, a villager, hired to wash out the trays we

My Early Years in Europe, Africa and Asia

ate off of in the mess hall. He plunged them into fifty-gallon cans of boiling water in order to wash them. He stood outside the mess hall and took our trays as we came out. We liked to joke with him. We would say something like, "You got boom boom (prostitutes)?" "Sure, got many good boom boom," he would answer with a grin. Where we were, there was not any such thing. You had to go into Da Nang for that, which I never did. I was recently married. But the jibing went on good-naturedly like that.

This old man enjoyed the small pay he got from us and refused to hand any of it over to the Viet Cong. So one day they cut off his thumb. He arrived at work with one hand bandaged up and got busy cleaning trays in the boiling water. He still refused to hand over any money to the VC, so three of them slipped into his village (the South Vietnamese district headquarters) right below our hilltop position one night, dragged him out of his hut, and put a bullet in his head.

Our colonel was furious. We all liked this guy. He was good-natured and a hard worker, not to mention courageous. So we imported a sniper from the regiment, and this guy took out one of the VC when they came into the village to renew their rice supply. I was corporal of the guard the night he did it, so I got the opportunity to look through his night vision scope. I was amazed at the lit-up green world it revealed. It was called a starlight scope then. A new thing. Now it is common.

To return to the keening women inside the battalion CP compound: they were there, and allowed to be there, inside the compound because they were wanting to collect solatium (solace) payments for their suffering. Those keening were not the principal victims. They were more distant relatives – say aunts or cousins. In the case of the child mentioned, the young mother was sitting on the ground alone a little distance away. She was not keening, but her pain was evident. It was these kinds of payments which were the principal business of the S5 (civil affairs) section of the battalion.

Mostly, during the early part of my sojourn with the battalion, we did not have any assaults on our firebase. That came later, on the night of November 7-8. I arrived in Vietnam on July 23, 1967. I left the battalion to transfer north in January, 1968. I believe I arrived in Phu Bai, a big "combat base," on January 13. The Tet Offensive took place a little over two weeks later. But that is another story.

Presently with the battalion, I made regular rounds to the various line units to deal with the matter of wounded and dead civilians. Another enlisted man, a lance corporal, was generally with me. He took care of the administrative details regarding solatium payments. I did the interpreting. On one such mission we went out to a CAP unit. A CAP is a combined action platoon. It usually had only about seven to nine Marines in it, one of them being a Navy corpsman. That is about half a squad.

They would be quartered in a village as a bulwark against Viet Cong activity. And they were supposed to be reinforced by South Vietnamese Popular Forces troops. But I never saw any of these troops. They were considered highly unreliable. So it was the little Marine unit on its own. In later years these units would move around at night, so the Viet Cong did not

My Early Years in Europe, Africa and Asia

know precisely where they were. But when I was there, they were less mobile. As can be easily discerned, these units were easy to wipe out.

There was one closer to the battalion CP that was wiped out, or, to be more precise, disappeared, during the Tet Offensive. The CAP unit I am presently referring to was located a fair distance from the battalion CP. They had a jeep, a radio, one or two machine guns (I only saw one, an M60), and their own personal weapons: M16 rifles. In those days these rifles were fully automatic, and there must be enough lead left behind in Vietnam to sink a battleship.

We were out there at that CAP unit on different occasions. On one, a Popular Forces soldier (which as I said, I never saw out there, except this one, after he was wounded and recovered) was wounded by a forty-five pistol. Hit in the chest too. It is amazing he survived. He and a Marine were goofing around Hollywood western style, and that is how he was wounded. At any rate, we made the solatium payment, which was hefty by Vietnamese standards. I think it was fifty dollars, the amount we gave out for the accidental death of a head of household or for the inadvertent demise of a water buffalo.

On another occasion I was standing and talking with a couple of officers (I do not remember why they were there), and that invited a sniper to try his luck. To fire the shot from concealment, he had to do it from a tree line across a rice paddy and therefore a fair distance away. His shot was a little to one side and low for the purpose. It hit a pile of rocks near our feet. The pile of rocks was for the local village women to wash clothes with. They pounded them into rags. There was a stream at the border of the rice field, next to the road. They washed clothes in that.

When the bullet hit, naturally we dove into the nearest ditch. A member of the CAP unit, on the other hand, ran out into the paddy where a machine gun was set up on a bunker. He raked the tree line, and that settled the matter. In truth, I suspect the sniper was already long gone. He would have to have been a fool not to have been.

However, when the bullet arrived and we dove into the ditch, I hauled out my forty-five and cocked it. It jammed with the round standing straight up in the chamber. For some reason, I found this very funny and literally rolled about in the ditch laughing. Everyone else thought they detected a spot of insanity. This was not the only time I did this, I am embarrassed to admit.

Once, coming back along Liberty Road with my lieutenant and two riders from the line companies, a front wheel flew off the jeep at fifty miles an hour. I managed to keep the jeep upright and on the road until it came to a stop, but afterward I burst into laughter. No doubt these fits of mirth on my part represented a release of tension. But the lieutenant did not see the humor in it.

One of our riders went out into the rice paddy and retrieved the wheel, and we somehow reattached it. I do not remember how, since all the lug nuts would presumably have been scattered and lost. As to the cause of the incident, it seems that a mechanic at the battalion CP with a clear dislike for me wanted to do me in. So he put the lug nuts on loosely. I did not know him. He seems to have thought I had too easy a job.

My Early Years in Europe, Africa and Asia

This particular village (the one guarded by the CAP unit) had other attractions. It was situated on the same river as the one which flowed past our command post. That is, it flowed past the base of the hill, Hill 37, which had been an old French fortification. Back to that in a minute. The reason I speak of the river now is that we had a bridge over it. So did the CAP unit. Later in the year, when the monsoon season arrived, the two bridges were destined to meet.

We were hit by a typhoon which had seventy mile an hour winds. It did not blow anything down at our CP, but it did wreak havoc with the tent flaps of the garrison tent draped over my hootch. In the morning we awoke to find the entire countryside under water, which rose to a level of neck deep (Vietnamese neck, that is). We brought a couple of villagers into the compound – a TB wasted old man and a boy with malaria – and kept them in a hootch under guard. None of the other villagers were interested in such intimate arrangements.

The point I am interested in now is that we, of course, made radio contact with that CAP unit. We were informed that their bridge had broken loose and was headed downriver to take out ours. It never did. It must have broken up on the way. But we also asked them why, since they had a jeep, they did not get out of there until the waters subsided. There was an extended pause on the other end of the transmission. Then the operator came back up and said in a low, serious voice, "Be advised, our jeep is also under water." Fortunately, there was a masonry-built French building in the village. They must have been on top of that.

George Lowell Tollefson

During the few days the water remained, we were supplied entirely by helicopter. We always relied on choppers to take out wounded, but now they brought us food and ammunition. These were usually supplied by truck.

Back to the CAP unit. At some point a couple of its members were accused of the rape of a village woman. Often these reports were instigated by the Viet Cong, but this one seemed to have some substance. Three of the members of that unit were transferred to the battalion CP to await further transfer to Division Headquarters for court marshal. They remained for several weeks. During that time, they were assigned two jobs. One was to pull fifty-gallon barrels out of the enclosed wooden shitter and burn their contents. Not a pleasant task. The other was to accompany the mine sweep units out on Liberty Road in the mornings to provide security for them.

When one is looking for and delicately removing mines, one cannot to be on the watch for Viet Cong at the same time. Such distractions are unhealthy. So that is what these three did, along with others. Members of the heavy weapons platoon supplied the bulk of the security, acting as riflemen for the purpose.

One of the three guys originally from the CAP unit was the Alaskan Indian who was wounded at the regimental CP observation post by a sapper-planted explosive charge. That is how I found out about it. Another was a guy who became friendly with me. As the battalion interpreter, I had developed lazy habits and occasionally got up a little later than the others in my hootch, all artillery forward observers, except for me.

My Early Years in Europe, Africa and Asia

So, after coming in from patrol, this person used to talk to me in the morning as I lay on my cot. One day he told me that they had gotten a new inexperienced and very gung-ho lieutenant as leader of the security contingent. He explained that that morning they had come under fire, and the lieutenant was shot in the head. He said this with a peculiar grin that left me with the impression that the lieutenant was fragged (which is not always done with a fragmentation grenade). Of course, I never sought to verify the situation. It was just my impression.

I should mention that our battalion CP, besides being on a hilltop position, was also an old French fortification of sorts. It had a low concrete parapet facing the river, which we would lie behind when firing back at the enemy during any of the numerous probing actions, which always occurred at night. The parapet was on top of a concrete underground bunker, which now served as the command operations center for the battalion. There were no other permanent structures, except for under the helicopter landing zone. Down there, through a hole in the ground barely large enough for a man to get through, was a holding cell.

I did not know it was there for quite a while, until one day a first sergeant from one of the line companies arrived with a Viet Cong prisoner. We put him down there, until he could be moved elsewhere. He was defined as Viet Cong. All I know is that he was supplying marijuana to some of the troops and was caught. VC did do this, but whether he was one of these or a profit monger I do not know. I doubt he was giving the stuff away.

George Lowell Tollefson

The first sergeant also had a young black Marine with him. This guy was the grenadier of a line company squad. Apparently, while out on patrol they had come under fire and had hit the deck in the paddy water. Then they moved forward. This guy remained where he was, and that was the problem. His job was to provide fire support with the M79 grenade launcher he was armed with. The first sergeant was very angry. He yanked the Marine out of his jeep and slammed him into the jeep in one motion. The young man would be sent to Division, where he would probably remain as a clerk.

After removing him from the vehicle, the first sergeant suggested to me that perhaps we could work together to start a little school teaching Vietnamese children English. I was not enthusiastic, and he did not pursue the matter. In spite of my occasional laziness, I did not think I would have time for such a project. I was not particularly impressed with the first sergeant either.

We had a Marine combat photographer who came through one day, and I was ordered to show him around in the village at the base of our hill. The photographer was new in country and wanted to get his feet wet. He would go on to do an extraordinary thing I would learn about later on. At this time, as we strolled about the village, he explained how a combat photographer does his business. I had suggested that he would be exposed to considerable fire. He said, no, troops were usually posed in a firing position and photographed in that way.

Well, that was not how it turned out. Quite awhile later, when I was with G2 (intelligence) at First Marine Division

My Early Years in Europe, Africa and Asia

Forward, or Task Force X-ray, at Phu Bai, he was passing through, and he just happened to be assigned to my hootch for the night. I had not seen him since that day in the village. I noticed that he had that long, vacant stare of one who has seen too much and asked him where he had been.

He told me that, among other places, he had recently been involved in the "hill fights" north of the Khe Sanh Combat Base. Contrary to what he had outlined in the village that morning many months before as his mission, he explained that he had experienced much of the fighting up close and had used his privilege of being able to exit the situation on any occasion when helicopters were taking out the wounded. But instead of leaving, he had used them to go from fight to fight.

He was not the only person like that. When I came back from R&R (rest and relaxation) in Hawaii, I met a guy at Division Headquarters, an interpreter himself, who was engaged in an argument with the Marine Corps (no doubt Division Headquarters, to which all interpreters administratively belonged, regardless of operational attachments). They judged that he had been wounded three times, and, according to established policy, that was an automatic ticket home.

As he was rolling up his blanket and fastening it to his pack in preparation to return to the field, he insisted to some of us that he had only been wounded twice because in a single action he had been simultaneously shot in the buttocks and hit in the hand by shrapnel. So that counted as one wound, as he saw it. I do not know what became of his situation because I had to get back out to the battalion the next day. He probably won his argument. The Marine Corps likes that kind of spirit.

George Lowell Tollefson

At the risk of getting even further out of sequence, which I have been doing anyway, I should mention some detainees we had. After the NVA attack on our firebase on November 7-8, we sent units out to clear and burn the surrounding villages involved in supporting the attack. That resulted in quite a few detainees, which we kept inside of a makeshift enclosure of concertina wire. They were fed boiled rice, which they squatted on their heels to eat. They were quiet, not knowing what would become of them, and over the treetops one could observe the silver flash of jets dropping ordnance and hear the boom and crash of its results. Black smoke was rising from the villages.

Into this – what was for her an unpleasant situation – came a representative of AID (Agency for International Development). She was neatly dressed, overweight, pink, and a little too delicate for the circumstances. A helicopter set her down, and out she came, disgusted at the mud that immediately engulfed her shoes and white socks. She could, of course, see the bombing, the smoke, and the sound of it, and she clearly found this quite displeasing. She also did not care much for the condition of the prisoners. Our own casualties the previous night were not her concern. She merely expressed her disapproval of the immediate situation, and the helicopter soon whisked her away.

About that time (I mentioned this in a short story some time ago when I wrote such things) a military six-by truck arrived with a load of captured rice. Some village women gathered around, and, when the men were unloading the truck, a bag fell and burst open on the ground. The women scrambled in and

My Early Years in Europe, Africa and Asia

gathered up as much as they could. As I may have mentioned before, war creates shortages of things like food.

That brings up another incident. At some point we retrieved an infant from some of the locals. For some reason, I associate this with the village the previously mentioned CAP unit was in. The child's parents had been killed by a mortar. Its aunt and uncle were taking care of it. But, as I said, food was in short supply, so they had not been feeding it. When we got hold of it, it was nearly dead. There was no flesh on its bones. What muscle there was was wrapped like cords around its arms and legs. It did die shortly after that. We had not discovered it in time.

That reminds me of my various medcap activities in the mornings. In one in particular, I remember the presence of wounded civilians. I cannot remember what actions had resulted in this, but among them was an old woman who had been struck in the head on one side by shrapnel. She was completely paralyzed on the opposite side of her body. Another casualty was a boy about the age of five. No relatives were with him. He did not whimper or make any fuss, but one of his hands was hanging on by a thin shred of cartilage. I took him up the hill to our compound and placed him into the arms of a crewman on a close-to-the-ground hovering helicopter that whisked him off to Da Nang and the very rustic civilian hospital there.

As I have mentioned, those medcaps were generally conducted by enlisted corpsmen. But the battalion aid station did have one doctor, and there was apparently also a dental technician. The dental technician, a black sailor, was in attendance one day. There was the usual line of civilians seeking medical care. They would generally say something like, "Toi bi dau hong," complaining of a sore throat or cold, and the corpsmen would give them a placebo. They were also given occasional shots for various reasons. I am not sure what these were.

Sometimes a village woman would arrive carrying or escorting a child covered with sores, usually on its head, flies in attendance. I remember once we told a mother to wash her child's head, and she was going to take it down to the river, a very brown and muddy river. We said "no, no, you need to use clean water." The corpsmen applied some sort of antiseptic paste to the sores in such cases.

Getting back to the dental technician on the only day I ever saw him, there was a woman in line who had a very pock-marked face. It was the result of shrapnel, I realized on observing her closely. But they were old, healed wounds. She was carrying a baby, and she was generously built. While she waited, lunch time rolled around, so she lifted her blouse and attached the child to one of her breasts. Our inexperienced technician's eyes grew as wide open as golf balls. No one else reacted.

On another occasion, the only one in my remembrance in which the doctor was present, a very pregnant woman came up and wanted him to examine her to determine how the fetus was doing. The doctor grew very excited, panicked I would say. He insisted, "Tell her I am not that kind of doctor." She would hear nothing of it, but kept insisting that he examine her. So finally he went into the building behind us and did so.

My Early Years in Europe, Africa and Asia

He probably told her the baby was fine: a placebo if ever there was one.

He was also the one who insisted that I get better control of the surging line by taking out my pistol and threatening the villagers. I do not believe in bluffs unless you have previously determined to carry them out, so I ignored his order. Fortunately, he was not a Marine officer and did not react to my insubordination.

Since I am on the topic of civilians, I think it is time to describe the civilian hospital in Da Nang. There was an incident where a young girl was wounded by a patrol. What happened was that she and her older sister were spotted crossing a rice paddy on one of its dikes. Unfortunately, the sister was carrying a rifle. That was a no no. Carrying a weapon meant you were a Viet Cong. So the patrol shouted at them, ordering them to halt. Instead, no doubt at the older sister's instigation, they started running. The patrol fired on them, killing the older sister and wounding the nine-year-old girl. The bullet passed through her cheek and neck. She was sent by medevac (medical evacuation) helicopter to the civilian hospital in Da Nang.

This was not a place you wanted to be. But it was what was available in that region. So one fine day the lieutenant and I went in to Da Nang to see how she was doing. When we arrived, we met a doctor on the first floor of the hospital, who conducted us up to the second floor where she was. We met him in the lab. There was not much there, to say the least. And the morgue was a separate, one room building outside where corpses lay stretched out in the heat and flies unattended.

George Lowell Tollefson

As we started our walk along the ground floor hall, I observed that there were villagers sitting on the floor all along both walls. Apparently a whole village. The doctor said the VC had mortared their village because they were not cooperating in some way. They were all silent. I noticed a woman holding onto a dead baby and another child in the arms of a dead woman. A number of them were smeared with dried blood. But, as I said, not a sound from any of them.

When we got upstairs, I saw that it was a long hall with rooms on one side and clouded up windows on the other. As we proceeded down this hall, we passed a large room full of wounded South Vietnamese soldiers. They were crammed in there on cots with no space between them. At the end of the hall was a closet. Inside the closet, perched on a small rug on her knees, was the little girl. Her wounds had healed, though the scars were plainly evident. I talked to her for a bit, and she recounted what I have already related. She did not seem upset, but there were tears in her eyes as she spoke of her sister. I think it was on the return from this trip that the incident with the recalcitrant wheel occurred.

I might as well continue in the same vein. One day a young woman came to us in tears wanting us to help her find her husband. Her husband had been a South Vietnamese Regional Forces soldier (one step down from the regular South Vietnamese Army and one step up from the Popular Forces). He was on an operation with some Marines when their patrol was ambushed: the usual bushwhacking from a dense tree line beside a rice paddy. This solder was severely wounded, and,

My Early Years in Europe, Africa and Asia

when the medevac choppers arrived, they took him out to the civilian hospital.

He was not heard of after that, and his wife was frantic to find him. We could not locate him, but the village grapevine eventually did. So the enlisted Marine I worked with and I climbed aboard a truck with a handful of villagers, including the young wife and the soldier's father, and headed for Da Nang. Of course, the soldier was not at the hospital. He had died and had been buried somewhere on the beach. Why there I do not know. But following the instructions people had gleaned from the village grapevine, we found the spot.

Several villagers got out of the truck and began digging in the sand. Soon they uncovered the body. It was greatly bloated, and the skin looked like thin plastic stretched tight. The villagers had a small vial of some sort of liquid that they put in their nostrils to quell the odor. I borrowed it and did the same. After they had uncovered the body, the young wife, who was waiting beside the truck with her father-in-law, suddenly got up and started running toward the grave.

I was standing a few yards back from the dig and saw her coming. I tackled her and returned her to the truck. What was she going to do? Jump in with him? He would have popped. As I said, he was greatly bloated. At any rate, I went back to the dig and fell to my knees. I was overcome by the emotion. Later, I felt embarrassed by that, but my fellow Marine never said a word about it.

When the body had been retrieved and put in a wooden box, the villagers loaded it onto the truck, and we headed back to the village. I was riding in the back with them. Along the way, we stopped and bought some soda pop, which was shared among them. But neither the father-in-law nor the wife took part in that or the conversation and joking that occurred as we headed home. They were silent, engulfed in their own grief and troubles. But the older man never showed any sign of emotion, unlike the young bride. She had only recently been married.

There was an incident with a platoon from one of our line companies. They were occupying a hill in dense jungle for the purpose of observing Viet Cong traffic. Unfortunately, they had not had time or the means to clear fields of fire on the side of the hill. So that made them quite vulnerable. They were only supposed to be there temporarily, but how long was not clear. There was also an Army gun crew with them. The crew was servicing a 175 millimeter howitzer. That was a big gun for those parts.

We were sent there in a jeep to investigate some civilian casualties from the night's fighting. The platoon had been overrun on the night before the morning we arrived. They had suffered casualties amounting to one third of the platoon, so they were very edgy when we got there. We initially stopped the jeep next to the big gun, not realizing they were in the process of executing a fire mission. As soon as I got out of the jeep, the gun went off, and the blast threw me against the jeep. It was deafening.

It seems that most of my experience in Vietnam was a conspiracy against my hearing in old age. This was especially true the first few months after I got to Phu Bai, when we were subjected to continual shelling.

My Early Years in Europe, Africa and Asia

After I recovered from the shock of the fire mission (it seemed to only involve one round), I proceeded into the middle of the tiny hilltop position with the lance corporal I worked with. We were told the wounded Vietnamese were in a village in the jungle at the base of the hill, and we were assigned a fire team, four men, to go down and check it out.

We proceeded down the hill, following a little Vietnamese girl. We were passing through tall elephant grass, and I in my occasional spaciness was tripping through the tulips, closely following the little girl. The lance corporal I worked with called out to me to slow down. I looked back, and he was quite a ways behind me. Even further back was the fire team. They were down on their haunches in the grass. It suddenly became clear to me that the little girl could be leading me into an ambush or a booby trap. So I took the cue and slowed down, behaving in a more alert manner.

When we got to the base of the hill, the elephant grass gave way to dense jungle, and just inside this was a hut which I assumed demarked one end of the village, though I saw nothing but it. This was where the girl had been leading us. Inside the hut were several wounded people. They explained that their wounds came from a mortar, one of ours that may have fallen short if the Viet Cong were not actually attacking from the village. The wounds were in their feet – in the soles of their feet. Apparently, they were sleeping, all facing the same way, when the mortar impacted nearby.

Villagers such as these did dig bunker holes under their beds to roll into when under fire, but these folks did not have time to react. They must have been wounded right at the beginning of the Viet Cong assault. If it was the VC. It may have been the NVA. They were increasingly active in the area. Sometimes they worked with the VC, sometimes separately. At any rate, my understanding is that by 1969, most Viet Cong members were North Vietnamese soldiers sent south to replenish their ranks. So much for an indigenous rebellion.

While I was in Washington, DC, attending language school I read a book by Che Guevara outlining the strategy of guerrilla warfare. According to him, it was to occur in three stages. First there would be local hit-and-run insurgent operations. Then this would progress to larger confrontations utilizing company-sized units. These would also be hit-and-run, but only after a good deal of casualty producing fighting. Finally, when the enemy was sufficiently demoralized, large regular army units would finish the job.

Well, this had to be modified in a conflict with a superpower with unlimited resources. So all three stages were employed at once. Mostly it was sniping and planting mines and booby traps by individual or small units. But it also involved much more intense confrontations with large combat units. And occasionally regular North Vietnamese Army (NVA) units were deployed from Laos into South Vietnam with tanks.

The North Vietnamese Minister of Defense, General Giap, was a resourceful guy. He fitted his available resources to his needs. In fact, it has often been said that the NVA buildup of several divisions for the siege of Khe Sanh was a feint designed to obscure preparations for the big Tet Offensive that was to simultaneously occur. To some extent that may be. But I think both operations were important to General Giap.

My Early Years in Europe, Africa and Asia

Whichever one worked best was good enough for him. Tired of an endless war and heavy bombing, he had all his cards on the table.

Though taken by surprise, the American forces were not daunted, and the communists suffered heavy losses in both cases. But these events turned the tide of public opinion in the United States, and this shift in attitude was greatly augmented by slanted news reporting, for the media by this time had become convinced that we were on the wrong path. I dare say they were right, but their dishonesty still stands, and it contributed greatly to the prejudicial attitude of the general public toward Vietnam veterans for decades to come. It is still our heritage, as the war has never been well understood.

I do not want to make it seem like there was always a lot of activity of one kind or another. War is often incredibly dull and boring. I remember sitting on the steps of a hootch one evening with some other guys and watching a firefight take place nearby in the dark. Perhaps it was the CAP unit nearby that eventually disappeared during the Tet Offensive. I do not know, but I do not think so. I was not aware of their taking any casualties then, and the battalion was responsible for them at the time. This was also a function of the S5, Civil Affairs section. But there were other units deployed in the vicinity. That is to say, one of our regular line companies had a platoon there. I visited them once, and they were in such a wet, swampy area, they had to distribute sandbags everywhere to walk on. God only knows where they slept.

Anyway, as we were leisurely observing the firefight, we saw a stream of tracers suddenly arc upward and realized someone had been hit and was falling backward. The tracers were red, not green, so we knew they were ours. There were many days like this, when we did little, but one always remembers the excitement. It provides the adrenaline that later can cause problems when a serviceman returns home.

Because one must always be alert for the unexpected – an ambush, a sniper, a booby trap, a mine – the intensity is always there. The result is that the entire countryside always seems brightly colored: lit up, one might say. Upon returning to the States, this is no longer the case, and everything seems comparatively dull, cast in endless uninspiring shades of gray. Eventually, most returnees adjust, but it is not an easy transition. It is why most veterans are always slightly alienated from an uncomprehending public.

And how do you answer questions like, how many people did you kill? As I mentioned before, I never shot anyone, but that does not mean I do not know what the experience of war is. It is an ugliness, and at the same time an excitement, I can never forget. To witness civilian death and suffering is unsettling, and to see your fellow American dead stacked like cordwood under blankets and the wounded awaiting medevac by helicopter is unforgettable.

One day, during a boring lull, we heard an explosion and several of us took off in a jeep to see what had happened. We did not go very far down a dirt road – all roads were dirt where we were – before we found a pile of twisted metal which had been a bus. There were people riding on top as well as inside the bus. They had been blown out into the surrounding rice fields. Quick as we went, by the time we got there the dead

My Early Years in Europe, Africa and Asia

and wounded had been removed or evacuated. But the patrol that came across them was still there, and that was the source of our information, other than the obvious evidence.

There was the unrecognizable pile of metal that had been the bus, and there was a huge crater in the road. The Viet Cong had planted a mine there intended for us, and instead it shattered the lives of a bunch of peasant farmers. People strategize and carry out wars, but war itself is indiscriminate. It is an uncontrollable wild beast and ought to be avoided whenever possible. But national leaders, often themselves untouched by war, are easily led into them on the basis of national vanity and so-called "honor."

It is the little things that count. Certainly those of us at the battalion CP had it better than those perpetually in the field. But the Marine Corps does not believe in luxury anywhere. We wore our combat boots and utility clothing until they wore out and were full of holes. In fact, we were proud of this. Going in to Division Headquarters covered with dust and looking a bit bedraggled made us stand out from the people there. For they were required to keep their boots polished and look reasonably neat.

I remember once being on my way to the disbursing office to get my pay and encountering a lieutenant colonel coming the other way. I hand saluted him, carrying an M16 that day, and he gave me the snappiest salute I ever received. I have to admit it felt good, though I am sure he thought I was from a line unit. Well, close enough.

Bathing at the firebase was a lark. Each evening before dark we would go down the hill toward the river at its base. There was a large plastic pool there and a pump filling it with water. We would shed our utility uniforms and stand naked in a line in front of a horizontal pipe outfitted with multiple holes. The water would be pumped out of the pool into the pipe and would shoot out the holes. There we bathed off the day's sweat and grime in plain sight of the village that was the district headquarters on the other side of the river. The river made a sufficient moat on that side of the hill, but it was not particularly wide. Oh well, the Vietnamese – in fact, anyone in the Far East – were not particularly concerned about nudity.

I shaved at the back of my hootch. There was a little wooden shelf that I set my gear on. I had a small piece of metal that I found somewhere. I could not clearly see my face in it, but I could barely make out the line of my jaw, and that worked out pretty well. Our restroom was a small wooden structure that contained several wooden seats on a wooden bench within. It was under these that the fifty-gallon cans were placed to be emptied of their contents in the morning. They were emptied by burning. It stunk, and the smoke was thick and black.

Next to the helicopter landing zone, a small shed with overhanging pipes was eventually built. We obtained a means of making hot water somewhere, and that was pumped into the overhanging pipes. At first it came out as steam and scalding drops of water. Not much fun. At any rate, it was mainly the officers who used it. They also had precedence when it came to evening volleyball. A net was set up at one end of the helicopter landing zone, and we were presumably invited to enjoy the sport when events permitted: first the officers, then the

My Early Years in Europe, Africa and Asia

enlisted. As it turned out, the officers almost inevitably played until sundown, so that generally precluded enlisted participation.

One night I decided to participate in an ambush patrol. It did not come to much, but it was interesting all the same. When we left the battalion command post loaded with grenades and our weapons, proceeding in a line going single file over the bridge that crossed the river, I had forgotten to load the chamber and put the safety on on my borrowed rifle. So, since it happened to be cocked, fortunately on an empty chamber, the bolt suddenly slammed home. You cannot imagine how loud that sounds when you are trying to slip out into the countryside after dark.

We finally came to a dense tangle of trees fronting two adjacent paddies which were at a ninety degree angle to each other. We set up there in an L-shaped ambush and waited in the heat and the mosquitoes. You could not slap at a mosquito out there. You had to be hospitable and let it suck, or brush it silently and very carefully away.

We were there for several hours. No Viet Cong resupply traffic. So finally a small pebble hit me, and I knew the squad leader had decided that it was time for us to head back to the compound. We did so. There were barking dogs, but I do not know if they were barking at us or something else. Hopefully no one else knew either.

There was an incident which I did not witness, but knew about. It took place at a bridge that had recently been blown by the VC and reconstructed. A small contingent of Marines was guarding it. It happened one day that there was a wedding celebration in the nearby village. The wedding procession arrived with the intention of crossing the bridge. For some reason, the corporal in charge was not amenable to the situation. He would not let them pass. This did not go over well with the priest heading the procession. He got into an argument with the corporal, and the corporal roughed him up in return. They were not going to cross his bridge.

This resulted in a complaint to the colonel, the battalion commanding officer, and the corporal was called in for a bit of chewing. It would appear that he had forgotten that we were there to win the hearts and minds of the people. This particular outlook was often forgotten by those who were taking casualties and suspected the complicity of the local village folk. It was certainly a delicate issue. Who was to blame and when? Hard to tell, always very hard to tell.

Speaking of incidents, I suppose one of the funnier ones involved the flare canisters. Whenever any action occurred, such as a probing action, the 81 millimeter mortar crew launched flares into the night sky. They swayed as balls of fire on their parachutes, and this made every bush, rock, and stick on the ground look like it was moving.

But most importantly, they had canisters associated with them. When the flare burst into radiance, these canisters began their whistling descent to the ground. You really did not want any of these flares to open directly above the compound, which sometimes they did. Then you had to listen to the scream of the falling canister and wonder where it would hit. One did punch a hole through the canvas cover of a hootch. It would have made a considerable dent in any person it hit.

My Early Years in Europe, Africa and Asia

Getting somewhat off the subject in this lighter vein, I am reminded of the R&R flights I took to Hawaii. I went on R&R twice because, unbeknownst to me, the clerks at Division Headquarters set it up in such a way that my first one was not recorded. We were all supposed to get one R&R somewhere in the midst of our tour. But in my eleventh month in Vietnam, when I was at Phu Bai, it was suddenly discovered that I had never been on R&R. Poor guy. Alas, not true. But that is when I discovered the ruse, and I have to admit that I did not inform anyone of the error.

That was close to two months before I returned to the States at the end of my tour of duty. The flights to and from Hawaii were surreal. I wore a standard dress uniform, as did all the other military passengers on the airliner, and the stewardesses were uniformly young, nice, and pretty. Out of the mud, sweat, and grime, this was quite a change. Frankly, it was Valhalla. And the return flight was, of course, depressing.

It is the flight back from the second R&R that I vividly remember. I was sitting next to a recently married young lance corporal who was a 60 millimeter mortar crewman stationed next to the DMZ (demilitarized zone). There was constant shelling and other emoluments there. A happy place. He did not think so. He still had half his tour to do, whereas I was near the end of mine. He brought down the tray in front of him and buried his face in a pillow all the way back on that flight.

I previously mentioned things happening near Hill 37 when nothing was affecting us. One morning VC were spotted planting a mine nearby on Liberty Road. Not a good thing to do in broad daylight. We had artillery on the hill. That is why it was called a firebase. So a mission was fired: three VT (variable timing) rounds, and these detonated over the heads of the VC. No more VC.

I have previously mentioned the night attack on our firebase, which occurred on the night of November 7-8, 1967. I did not know, but fortunately our S2 (intelligence) section knew what was coming. Where they got their information I do not know. Perhaps from a POW, captured documents, or from observations of enemy troop movements and resupply operations. I do not know. But the S2 knew we would be hit that night by a regimental strength North Vietnamese Army unit.

If I remember correctly after all these years, it was the R144th NVA Regiment. They assaulted us from the river, which means the steep side of the hill, which was quite steep. This is peculiar because the other side of our wire perimeter was approached by fairly level terrain. But there was a village on that side which was unfriendly toward us. Obviously that means it was friendly toward the communists. The village never directly bothered us, and we never bothered it. Likewise, the enemy never approached us from that more convenient side. To do so would have drawn an immense curtain of fire from us, and probably would have decimated the village.

So they came at us on the steep side. They came in mass, initiating their attack with a mortar barrage. What I did not know was that there were three helicopter gunships on the LZ (landing zone), waiting for this to happen. It is surprising that I did not know because my hootch was the second one down from the LZ. At any rate, when the assault began with the barrage and the mass movement of troops toward us, we came

My Early Years in Europe, Africa and Asia

out of our hootches, boots, helmet, and rifle in hand, and dove into the bunkers next to them, where we quickly pulled on our boots, slapped the helmets on our heads, and headed for the perimeter.

The bunkers were square structures with sandbag sides and no tops, easy to dive into. The attack began at two in the morning. Such things almost always did, so the enemy would have time to approach and withdraw under cover of darkness. The purpose of the mortars was to keep our heads down while the NVA troops moved toward the hill. But they were also directed toward the ammunition dump in the hope of blowing it up. The communists always walked their mortars over a position, going from one end of it to the other. This eliminated the need for adjusting their fire.

As this was occurring, the gunships took off and positioned themselves directly over the advancing NVA. One of them turned on a spotlight. The other two canted over onto their sides and circled the one with the spotlight. As they did so, their gunners fired their machine guns into the troops below, lines of red tracers marking their fire. At the same time, Marines were firing from the perimeter of the compound, a small part of which was lined with the concrete parapet previously mentioned. Also, a reaction platoon made up of mechanics and cooks was sent down into the fray.

When the people in my hootch first dove into the bunker, along with me, they exchanged a few brief words, such as, "Where is so and so?" "He is still in the hootch." Then, all of them being forward observers, they headed for the command operations center to direct counter mortar fire against those shelling us. So in an instant I was alone.

I jumped out of the bunker and ran back to the door of the hootch. I pulled the tent flaps apart. It was pitch black, and I could not see anything inside. The only thing I could see in my peripheral vision was the flashes of the mortars going off around me. I knew that guy was still in there, so I started yelling, "Incoming! Incoming! Incoming!" No response. So I dove back into the bunker.

From there I saw our ammo technician gathering up ammunition to haul to the perimeter. I ran over to help him. We lugged cases of ammunition up to the men on the perimeter. The gunships were still firing their tracers into the troops below. When it was over, we discovered that only one NVA soldier had made it up to our wire. He was lying dead on our wire – no doubt a sapper.

Our casualties were four dead and about twenty-five wounded. In the morning, the wounded were lying and sitting on the LZ, depending on the condition of their wounds. Several of them had IV bottles strapped to the volleyball net which was strung across one end of the LZ. Helicopters were coming in and out, taking out the wounded. The dead were stacked over to one side next to a hootch. They were covered by blankets. Trucks would take them in to Da Nang later.

One of those dead had been in the reaction platoon that went down to engage the NVA. No doubt some of the wounded were in that platoon as well. The mechanic who later misrigged the front wheel on my jeep was also in that reaction platoon. He was angry about those of us who were not in the

My Early Years in Europe, Africa and Asia

platoon. He expressed his views when he delivered the jeep to me, but I did not realize how serious he was.

Another KIA (killed in action) was a young black truck driver who had delivered his load too late to return to Division. So he stayed overnight. When the stuff hit the fan, he did not know to move quickly to the bunker to don his gear. That is something you learn to do in your sleep. He sat up on his cot to pull on his boots and was hit by a piece of shrapnel that came through one canvas side of the hootch and penetrated his back, entering his heart.

The CAP unit near us was also hit, and they were the source of the other two dead and some of the wounded. The next morning the guy who had remained in my hootch came to me and asked me to accompany him to the bridge to fire a few rounds from our pistols. Forward observers also carried pistols. Shooting into the river was not considered a waste of ammunition. It was necessary to prevent anything explosive from approaching the bridge.

While we stood on the bridge and expended a few bullets, the guy told me he had frozen when things started and could not move. So here was a perfectly experienced guy who probably already had his share of exposure under fire and who had now had a moment of hesitation, never to be repeated. That is the way of such things. Telling me this, he was in effect thanking me for attempting to get him out of the hootch the night before.

We had a lance corporal with us at the battalion who was a combat correspondent. He would often be sitting at the front of my hootch writing out his stories. I observed him there once, with a sheet of paper on a small box, writing by candlelight just inside the hootch entrance. The candle had bent and fallen over in the heat and gone out.

His stories would be published in the Stars and Stripes newspaper, a military journal. He was known to exaggerate, and his news articles had become something of a joke among us. I later heard that in this case he reported many enemy dead scattered over our wire. Always good for a laugh. There were plenty of enemy dead, but only one of them made it up to the wire.

Once I had a conversation with him when we were on "hole watch" together. The "holes" were bunkers partially dug into the ground and positioned at intervals along the perimeter of the compound, most of them on the river side, since the attacks always came on that side and we understood why. Of course, there were bunkers on the other side – just not as many.

The night the correspondent and I were together, it was raining, and we were sitting on top of the bunker, since the inside was a pool of water. These bunkers were more complex sandbag and wooden beam structures with tops on them and firing apertures inside. The insides were rarely used, especially in the rainy season.

So there we were in our ponchos, our rifles (mine borrowed) under our ponchos, the rain pouring down the ponchos onto our boots. There were three of us, and the other guy was asleep. Usually only one would be awake, taking his turn at watch. But this time we were both up, and we were discussing the war in general terms.

My Early Years in Europe, Africa and Asia

The correspondent expressed his view of the people. He had never been in that part of the world before, and he thought the people were ridiculously primitive, shall we say subhuman. That is a viewpoint that helps in the killing business. So he asked me, "Have you ever seen a wheelbarrow over here?" I said, "No." He responded, "Well, keep shooting."

I went on my first R&R within about a week after this attack. When I came back, the lance corporal I worked with told me that there had been a second attack and the five men guarding the bridge had been killed. These men had been transferred from line companies to the bridge assignment because they had only a month left of their combat tour. It was supposed to be a little safer.

It seems that most American casualties in Vietnam occurred in the first and last month of a person's tour. The first month because he was green, like I was. And the last month because he would become overconfident and careless. In the case of the men guarding the bridge, they were just unlucky. But it is surprising people were not killed there in the first attack. I think the NVA crossed the river the first time in sampans (small boats) and ignored the bridge.

When Thanksgiving rolled around, we celebrated with a big can of Spam. It was in a long, green, square can, about a foot long and four inches square, so it must have been a C ration. Our scrounger, who was the S4 (logistics) sergeant, had traded a box of combat knives to the Navy for a case of beer, and had traded that to the Air Force for the large can of Spam. I may have the Navy and Air Force backward in this deal. I was not involved in the transaction.

George Lowell Tollefson

This may seem to have been an uneven trade – a bunch of good combat knives for a can of Spam – but it was Thanksgiving, and this was our turkey. It was great. I still eat Spam sometimes in remembrance of this occasion. It was just those of us in the S4 and S5 that enjoyed this feast.

Later there was a Christmas truce. The idea behind this was that the enemy would suspend its activity, and we would suspend ours. But we knew they would conduct resupply operations, so we had patrols out watching their movements. Normally these would have been ambush patrols, but now they were simply observation patrols, using the same methods as the ambush patrols but not engaging anyone in combat.

At the CP, we were given a ration of two cans of beer each on Christmas Day. Since some guys did not drink the beer, including myself on this occasion (or maybe I did have some – I cannot remember), others had enough to get high. We also received a bunch of Red Cross care packages. They arrived in an Army spotter plane, a little prop job (a Cessna or something like that), which dropped them as it passed over the hill.

One of the orders for anyone entering the CP was that he had to immediately unload his weapon. No loaded weapons inside the CP, except when the CP was under fire. It was something I frequently neglected to do, and I was usually immediately reminded by someone. I mean within seconds of my entering the compound. How I could forget so often, I do not know, but it fits my profile.

As for people getting high on the extra beer, there was one guy in my hootch who did so and who was quite upset about something – the war in general, I suppose. It is true that the

My Early Years in Europe, Africa and Asia

cease fire was eerie. Sudden silence when there is always gunfire and artillery or bombs booming in the surrounding countryside is unnerving. We all felt it. But this guy was tanked up.

Most of the guys in the hootch were playing cards or just relaxing. This guy came in wound tight. He started cussing and yelling cute little four letter word epithets about Vietnam and the craziness of being there. No one would have paid much attention to that, but he pulled out a loaded pistol and waved that around as he carried on. Needless to say, several guys tackled and disarmed him.

That was Christmas for you. It was a relief when the truce ended. Christmas was also the only time I remember the S5 doing something sugary. A bunch of other Red Cross style care packages were brought in by truck, and our job was to distribute them to the natives. As if the villagers, most of whom were not Christians, would understand the meaning of good will and peace toward all attached to these packages. Hell, I did not understand it, given the context. But we did our duty and handed the stuff out to a bunch of kids. I do not remember what village we were in. The hamlets were all strikingly similar, except that the district headquarters did have some permanent buildings in it.

One day in early January, 1968, the major who was my interpreter/translator team leader arrived in a jeep for the express purpose of seeing me. I think it was the only time he was outside of Da Nang. He arrived with his shiny gold leaf rank insignia blazing in the sun on his collar and was politely reminded by someone that it was not a good idea to sport such things where he was. We normally wore black rank insignia. Harder for snipers to distinguish choice targets. He quickly removed his.

His message for me was to "ask" me if I wanted to go north with him. He and I did not get along, and I knew he was ordering, not asking. So I agreed to do so. I have to admit that the S5 had just gotten a new lieutenant who was unpleasantly gung-ho. I did not want to serve under him, so the arrangement was convenient. I left the battalion within a few days after the Major returned to Da Nang.

My Early Years in Europe, Africa and Asia

Vietnam: Phu Bai

For many years I have considered this decision a mistake because, when the Tet Offensive occurred a few weeks later, I was no longer with the battalion. I felt I should have been there. But time mellows one over the years, and a good many of those have passed since then. I realize that, while being a pogue (not on the front lines) in G2, Division Forward at Phu Bai was unpleasant, I did learn a great deal there, which helped me to better understand the war.

Besides, being subjected to shellfire several times a day in February, tapering off gradually into May, provided its own degree of excitement. The shellfire was a combination of mortars and rockets. The only time it was artillery was when the South Vietnamese Army got its coordinates mixed up. That happened once.

The shellfire began with the Tet Offensive, coming in with a density of around a hundred twenty or thirty rounds at a time. Of course, I did not count them each time, but there always seemed to be plenty of rounds while it lasted. The first few days they hit us three or four times a day. Then it settled into twice a day, oddly enough at two o'clock in the afternoon and two o'clock in the morning. This was February. It gradually tapered off after that.

It was much later that I learned how it was possible for this to go on for so long when Marine patrols would obviously be looking for the source. It was probably sometime in May that I received a call on a field phone while I was on duty (a twelve hour shift seven days a week) from the pilot of an Army spotter plane. I normally sat behind a row of such phones with other Marines in the command operations center in a partially underground fortified bunker. My assigned phone was the G2 (intelligence) phone. The pilot told me to go up to the big map on the wall, so I did. He then reeled off a number of coordinates which I marked with pins. These points demarcated a long line of deep trenches extending from Hue City around Phu Bai and extending into the jungle south of Phu Bai.

When the Tet Offensive started, the North Vietnamese Army simply marched into the unguarded city of Hue, the ancient capital of Vietnam. It took the Marines and the South Vietnamese Army a month to clear the city of them, as they were well entrenched. When this was finally accomplished, the NVA simply disappeared. No one knew what became of them, until these trenches were discovered by the spotter pilot. Then the manner of their escape not only became clear, but it was also obvious how they were able to shell us so regularly for so long. Not long after the discovery of the trenches, or perhaps at the same time, a Marine company ran into a NVA regimental base camp in the jungle and was pinned down. Reinforcements were sent in to get them out of there. These NVA regulars were probably the ones who had been in Hue.

I have not mentioned how I got up to Phu Bai, which was about sixty miles north of Da Nang. I went from the battalion CP into Da Nang, where I learned that the First Marine Division Headquarters was planning to move to Phu Bai. They

My Early Years in Europe, Africa and Asia

began this move by setting up a division forward in Phu Bai, called Task Force X-ray, under a brigadier general. I was part of that move. But I was a peon, so my mode of transportation was a crowded C130 cargo plane, the kind that has a big hatch like the mouth of a bullfrog at the rear end of it.

I and a bunch of other enlisted Marines were crammed into the fuselage like flies into the belly of that frog on a hot summer day. It was definitely hot that day. We were herded into the body of the plane and ordered to bunch it up tight "asshole to bellybutton." We had all our gear: helmets, rifles, etc. I do not remember anything about packs or sea bags. But they must have gone up with us. After we were crammed in as tight as possible, the rear jaw of the plane was closed.

The plane revved up for takeoff. It got very hot inside. Sweat was pouring off us. When the plane jerked into a taxi down the runway, we all fell over in one mass, rifles jamming into backs and ribs. We could not get back up. No room to maneuver. So that is how we traveled from Da Nang to Phu Bai.

After we landed, we were disembarked and loaded onto trucks and taken to the area of our hootches. It was the rainy season, and the combat base was wet and muddy. When I jumped off the truck (I had my sea bag at this point), I sank nearly to my knees into the mud on the road in front of my hootch.

Welcome to Phu Bai, a place of mud, rats, rockets, mortars, and, eventually, blown up hootches and mess hall. None of the destroyed structures were rebuilt while I was there. The Marine Corps liked it that way. The mess hall had lost its seating area, which was blown away by a rocket. But the serving line and galley were intact, so that was good enough.

We would stand in the rain about seventy meters from the mess hall, wounded men in the line with white bandages on their heads and elsewhere. A sergeant standing at what had been the door, which was now gone, would signal holding up one hand with fingers extended. Five of us at a time would move up to the mess hall and progress down the serving line with food trays or mess kits extended.

The trays had separate compartments, but it was traditional in those days to use only the center compartment, which was the largest. The serving guys would ladle the food into that compartment: first, say, a Salisbury steak, then powdered mashed potatoes on top of that, then green beans on the potatoes, and finally canned peaches on top of the green beans.

Leaving the mess hall after getting our trays filled, we would head for the nearest row of hootches to find a place to sit and eat. Fortunately the row of hootches next to the mess hall had tin roofs. I do not remember if they all did in that row or just a few. Anyway, we would sit against the outside of the hootch with our knees drawn up and the trays or mess kits balanced on them. This would get most everything but our boots and the bottoms of our utility trousers out of the rain, which was running off the tin roof. After eating, we returned to a set of fifty-gallon cans with boiling water in them and washed our trays or mess kits in them. This was well into the month of February, after the mess hall had been redesigned by a rocket, but it lasted the rest of the time I was there.

My Early Years in Europe, Africa and Asia

One peculiar thing I remember is a fact I observed one day. The hootches all around my hootch remained intact, but the next row out in a circle around my hootch was demolished. It made me feel blessed, but it was also rather strange. Coincidence? It is not for me to know. The stuff hits the fan in its own peculiar way. I have no say in it that I am aware of.

I should point out that the Tet Offensive occurred on the next to last day of January, about two and a half weeks after I arrived in Phu Bai. I arrived on January 13, if I remember correctly. Most people know about this offensive. It was a military defeat for the communists. But due to slanted news reporting, it put an end to any appreciable public support for the war.

Nevertheless, the war managed to continue for several more years. President Nixon conducted a farcical withdrawal of US troops from Vietnam and a bombing of the North in a process of "Vietnamization," and Le Duc Tho and Henry Kissinger received the Nobel Peace Prize for conducting equally farcical negotiations toward ending the conflict. The war ended as the communists had always had in mind, so when the conditions were right, that is when it ended. Period.

For years after the war reached its grand finale in April, 1975, many of the older generation were of the opinion that those of us in Vietnam did not fight as well as they had. Well, it was a different kind of war, and, as I may have mentioned before, there were limitations on what we could do. But it did not help that the news media picked the most demoralized American units in Vietnam to create a picture of broken discipline with such things as combat refusals and blowing marijuana smoke down the barrels of rifles. These were far from the norm, as far as I can see. Most troops did their duty, albeit with a growing awareness that it was a lost cause.

I say to the previous generation, most of them gone now: try fighting your war against so much public hostility and a general lack of moral support both during and long after the conflict. It was a sick situation, and the worst of it was biased and downright dishonest reporting. In addition, we have not learned anything. The US is still nation building. We still think we are the world's fairy godmother and we can wave our magic military and economic wand and set the world to rights according to our enlightened vision. Even with the mess in Iraq and our withdrawal from Afghanistan, I wonder if we have learned anything.

Some personal memories of the shelling: The most important fact about chronic incoming fire of the large, noisy, destructive kind is that you learn to respond to it in your sleep. You grab your utility trousers, boots, helmet, weapon, etc., rush out, dive into the four-sided, waist high bunker (sometimes, but not always, with no top), and wake up pulling your boots and trousers on and getting your helmet onto your head.

That is, you do this if you have not already done it on the way out of the hootch (not a good way to do it) and if you are not lying flat on your face in the bunker in the lowest profile position you can assume. But if a 122 millimeter rocket hits the bunker, your position is not likely to matter, so not everyone is lying on his face.

Once I remember not being near a bunker when the stuff came in, so I dove into a muddy ditch and crawled into a culvert. As the sky roared with the incoming, deafening explosions occurring all around, and the ground shaking repeatedly, I could feel rats racing over my legs. They were upset too.

On another such occasion, when I was far from my hootch, in came the rockets and mortars, and I dove into the nearest bunker. I was the first one in there, but the occupants, arriving immediately after my entry, were quite hospitable. We were, after all, all in the same boat. It was quite a fancy bunker. Not only did it have a top. It had two lengthy covered entrances. Lovely, lovely, an architectural wonder for the Marine Corps. We were not usually creative in relation to bunkers and fighting holes. Whatever was functional would do.

Being first, I, of course, ended up in the middle. There was a large puddle there, and I sat in this. The others clambered in on both sides. Perhaps partly because of me, it was very crowded, and we were squeezed in tight. Naturally the banging and booming went on outside, and you hoped for no direct hit. Imagine the amount of human hamburger that bunker would have supplied.

I felt reasonably calm, but I must have been aware of adverse possibilities because I went to sleep. When I woke up, the all-clear siren was blaring, and I was the only one in the bunker. I crawled out and went about my business. Falling asleep, along with hysterical laughter, seems to be my way of dealing with stress. We all have our means.

On another occasion we were in a bunker lying on our faces. Not the bunker next to my hootch, if I remember rightly. At any rate, the guy behind me had a hold on my ankles. Every time a crash and a boom occurred, he squeezed them very tightly. It was painful. But I never said anything. Nevertheless, the next morning while sitting in the hootch, he suddenly ripped into me, saying that I had never had any rough experiences such as he did. He apparently served as part of the perimeter guard. I did not respond. I usually do not.

On yet another occasion, our sergeant major came around and ordered us to tear down every other bunker, leaving the alternate ones for protection. We were to dig them into the ground. The present ones were on the surface. So we did as ordered and discovered, not surprisingly, that the water table was just a few inches below the surface. What exactly are sergeant majors for? I was never sure.

That night the torn down bunkers remained torn down. So, when the inevitable two a.m. shelling occurred, I woke up running in a circle around a single sandbag which was lying on the ground where the bunker had been. The only other person in the hootch at the time was following me, running around in the same circle just behind me. We both woke up at the same time and ran over to the bunker still standing catercorner to us.

About midway through my time in Phu Bai President Johnson gave his speech declaring that he would not run for a second term as president. I heard it on someone's transistor radio, which was tuned to the armed forces station. Of course, that announcement was a surprise, though not a complete surprise. Martin Luther king was assassinated about that time, and Senator Robert Kennedy would soon be shot. There were riots as well as the usual mass demonstrations against the war in the cities. We often wondered if we were in the right war.

My Early Years in Europe, Africa and Asia

At any rate, my immediate reaction was to think: "That is nice. You can quit, but we cannot."

My introduction to Phu Bai had not been a good one. I was a little out of sorts about having been removed from the familiarity of the battalion and introduced into a clerical world I did not want to be in. Nevertheless, I did as I knew I should. When I first arrived at Phu Bai, part of Division Forward had already been set up, so I was introduced to a sergeant who was about to rotate back to the States. He had been doing what I was about to do and would be showing me the ropes.

Unfortunately, he was a bit sarcastic and sharply informed me that I knew nothing about intelligence. He was right, but I bristled and responded: "Well, at least I have been shot at." It was definitely the wrong thing to say. The result was that he never explained anything to me, and he did his best to poison the well for me with the officers who were my superiors. This came to a head after he had gone and things had heated up.

There was a captured 122 millimeter rocket that I was informed of. It had identifying numbers on it, and I failed to report it up the ladder to the G2 colonel. As a result, Saigon got wind of it before the colonel did. The ball rolled downhill from the general to the colonel. Naturally, I got into trouble for that and began to pay greater attention to details afterwards. On the job training.

But this was not the colonel's only problem. He had a corporal or lance corporal whose' duty it was to keep all the intelligence records for him. But it was entirely on file in this guy's head, and when he rotated back to the States, it was discovered that his file cabinet was empty. In effect, the colonel had no memory of important details concerning the enemy at a time when the enemy was quite active in his sector.

The battle for Hue City was protracted for a month. During the Tet Offensive, the NVA marched in in formation and took over. This was reported by a CIA operative who escaped with others through the drainage tunnels. Twelve hundred South Vietnamese civilians who worked for the CIA and various other governmental officials did not get out. They were rounded up by the NVA soldiers and summarily executed. They were beheaded and their bodies and heads buried in separate mass graves. These were discovered later by patrols in the area.

The Marines had quite a time of it in the sector of Hue they were assigned to retake. It seems the NVA were well entrenched with machine guns set up at every street intersection, providing heavy fire down each thoroughfare. When the Marines tried to advance down these streets, they suffered heavy casualties and had to withdraw.

It seems that the Second Battalion of the Fifth Regiment was a major unit responsible for this operation. Their commander, a lieutenant colonel whose name I do not recall, finally realized that the Marine Corps had fought in jungle terrain for so long they had forgotten how to fight in a built up urban area. So he went back to Phu Bai, eight miles south of Hue, and began pouring through old manuals. Finally he discovered one that explained the situation.

He returned to Hue and ordered his troops to progress through the buildings. Thereafter they moved up the streets by blowing holes in the walls of buildings and so passing from

My Early Years in Europe, Africa and Asia

one to the next under relative cover. In this way they were able to suppress the machine gun emplacements and get control of the city.

Then suddenly the NVA melted away. That is when they used the trench network I have described to slip south undetected. I do not think I remember the details of the street fighting from when I was in Phu Bai. I may have, but I am not sure. More likely, I read about it later in the States. Whatever is the case, I have mentioned it because I think that colonel should be remembered for his actions. People simply doing their job like this are often overlooked. So one more mention of the fact may help it to stick. But then again, maybe not. That is the usual way of things.

During the battle of Hue, I remember the three star general in command of the Third Marine Amphibious Force (the command in charge of all Marines in Vietnam) paying us a visit. He and our one star general were discussing matters in front of the big map. I was sitting as usual in front of one of the bank of field phones facing them. It seems they could not get tanks down the narrow streets in Hue. And they were reluctant to use aircraft in support of the infantry fighting there. This was because the city of Hue was sacred to the Vietnamese and could not be severely damaged or destroyed. So it was decided that the infantry would have to slug it out unassisted, which they did.

Speaking of our one star general, this reminds me that the reason I know how the CIA operatives got out of Hue and how the NVA initially entered into it is that the general debriefed these people in a little room off to one side of the main room of the command operations center where I sat. The door to the debriefing room was left ajar as they discussed the matter.

Also, in a hallway behind the main room was a little room that was the communications center. This is where the radio operators were. One day, passing by, I overheard some very agitated radio chatter. It seems that a reconnaissance team had been surrounded and ambushed in the jungle. As they spoke over the radio, their dead and wounded were piling up. You could hear the panicked excitement in their voices.

They must have been in the high canopy rain forest. There was a helicopter overhead, but it could not see them. The members of the small recon team used a strobe light to indicate their position to it, but it could not land. So it found an open landing spot some distance away, and the team was notified that it would have to fight its way to that landing zone in order to be extracted. They did do this and were taken out.

The major who was the team leader for my dispersed interpreter/translator team was functioning at Phu Bai as the assistant G2. What he seemed to have actually been doing was combining intelligence sources to decide on where to direct the day's H&I fire. This is harassment and interdiction fire. Its purpose is to disrupt enemy troop movements and other such activity.

He would go over aerial photographs and compare these to intelligence information gleaned from sources listed as reliable, usually reliable, occasionally reliable, generally unreliable. Out of this came the day's artillery fire missions. These locations were usually in areas where we did not have a solid presence and the enemy did. But, of course, there were also

My Early Years in Europe, Africa and Asia

villages in these places. So civilian casualties must have been high in comparison to military casualties.

One day as I was passing by in the wooden building next to the COC (command operations center) bunker, the major spotted me and started proudly explaining his activities to me. I did my best to be attentive and properly impressed, but I could not help but reflect on the likelihood of high civilian casualties. Some people had the attitude that these villagers were supportive of the communists, and I do not doubt that they were. But did they have a choice? The communists were in control of their area. And were these casualties necessary, given the relatively little harm that was probably meted out to the enemy?

To this day I have retained the view that we rely too much on heavy firepower. Sometimes it can be argued that it is necessary to save the lives of our own troops, and nobody can argue against that. But is it always necessary, or are we often a bit careless about the administration of this rather potent preventive medicine? It is not an easy thing to determine, and battlefield conditions are not conducive to gentle methods or a soft touch.

At one point during my time at Phu Bai, I accompanied a convoy of captured weapons to Da Nang. Many of these weapons were new and still encased in their Cosmoline jelly. The gel is a rust and corrosion inhibitor. We were hauling truckloads of these weapons south. For some reason, I remember this convoy as proceeding north, but that makes no sense. All of these captured weapons would have come from the fighting in and around Hue and around and south of Phu Bai. They would have been gathered up by Division Forward, which was the headquarters for the battle of Hue City and other operations in the area. That is why we were shelled for so long. Having gathered the weapons up, we would then have transported them south to Division Headquarters for further intelligence analysis.

So I was sent along as part of the security. We traveled down one of the few paved roads in this part of Vietnam at the time. That is to say, part of it was paved. I believe the road, running close to the coast, was an extension of Highway One, a main conduit running north and south. At about halfway through the sixty mile journey, we passed some US Army engineers working on the road, and they told us that the Viet Cong were active in the area. Shortly after this, the front of the convoy was hit.

I was riding shotgun (that is, not driving and with my borrowed rifle loaded and the safety off), and the front of the convoy had gone around a bend. There were brush jungle covered hills lining the road, so I could not see around the bend. There was an explosion and a puff of black smoke followed by gunfire, particularly the familiar pop and rattle of M16s. The convoy stopped, and the driver and I jumped out of the truck and dove for cover on the side of the road. All the other trucks did the same. The gunfire ceased, and we were ordered back into the trucks, so we proceeded cautiously forward.

When we rounded the bend, I could see a little way ahead of us to where some men were gathered. As we approached them, a lieutenant came up to the truck and told us to keep

My Early Years in Europe, Africa and Asia

moving. There were wounded and some dead on the side of the road with a corpsman and several Marines gathered around them. The lieutenant told us that the VC who had ambushed the convoy were being pursued into the brush jungle covering the hills. We continued onward to Da Nang without further incident.

Well, the convoy took place after the shelling of Phu Bai had stopped, and it was the last bit of excitement I would encounter in my tour. The shelling stopped sometime in May after the discovery of the trenches, as I said, and, until the time I left at the beginning of August, nothing further whatsoever happened. It was a long couple of months. At the end, I went south and waited with other grubby Marines for a plane out of Vietnam. This soon occurred, but we were not flown to the United States. We were grubby, and all had attitudes. So we had to be civilized at least enough to present ourselves to the world stateside.

This was accomplished in three days in Okinawa by having us change into clean, neat uniforms (not utility clothes) and shined boots (not jungle boots, badly scuffed or with holes in them). We were then marched around until we got used to being in formation and responding automatically to the kinds of orders that characterized a garrison Marine. Then we were shipped home on an airliner: a direct jet flight with comfortable seats and pretty, young stewardesses. It was not like the trip in a C130 with all our gear, including a jeep, that took three days to get to Vietnam. We then sat along the walls of the fuselage, staring at the gear and eating box lunches, spend-

George Lowell Tollefson

ing a night in Hawaii and a night in Guam before arriving at Da Nang.

My Early Years in Europe, Africa and Asia

Stateside

So ended my long sojourn in Asia. I had been there off and on since the age of ten. I was now twenty-two. My years in the States would turn out to be an intense and often confusing struggle to realize my potential as a writer. I had been captivated by Hemingway's novel, *For Whom the Bell Tolls*, in my senior year in high school, and this had a lot to do with my joining the Marines in the first place.

Eventually, after my divorce from my first wife, I completed my formal education. We had had a son and a daughter by then. They were ages four and two when I left. Many things were the cause of my leaving, and I will not go into them, though I must admit that I did not leave her in a pleasant way. The divorce and my subsequent absence was undoubtedly rough on the kids, but I had to go, as I believed, to save the integrity of my mind, which is a hard thing to explain. Impossible, in fact.

But the proper development of my mind has always come first with me, and it was, of course, not understood by her. Nor is it understood by most people. For they are not driven by a sense of having to do something. I was not sure what, but I knew it was connected with my writing, so I struggled on for years, trying to realize it. As I mentioned before, I did not, in my opinion, pass completely out of my adolescence until the age of sixty, so it was a long journey.

George Lowell Tollefson

Over time, I did finish my formal education – at least, as far as I was going to go with it. It was not until I was thirty that I set foot for the first time on a university campus. That was at Boise State University, where I obtained a bachelors degree in English literature in two and a half years. The reason for the short duration of this effort was that I had received sixteen semester credits for my year long Vietnamese language and physical training in the military. That encouraged and spurred me on to complete a number of CLEP (college level examination program) tests, and these along with the other credits shortened my tenure there.

I graduated magna cum laude, so that encouraged me to enter graduate school at the University of Washington two years later to study philosophy. In this endeavor I completed a masters degree, but did not remain to obtain a doctorate. I value my time there, but logical positivism and language analysis held dictatorial sway over universities throughout the country, and to this day I intensely dislike this emphasis. Most of my professors were not positivists, but still it was the dominant influence. So I left with the masters, deciding to pursue a literary ambition.

Eventually this resulted in one hundred and sixty short stories and three short novellas, before my mother's death in 2000 caused inner turmoil and eventually a rerouting of my efforts. I taught philosophy at the University of New Mexico's Valencia campus for five and a half years, doing alternate summers as well as the regular semesters. This was from January, 2006, to May, 2011, and it was during this time that I discovered my deep love for philosophy.

I was able to think about it on my own away from the influence of the prevailing academic fashion. Over the years, an independent system of thought had matured in my mind, much of the process unconscious. It is with this change that I found my true purpose and finally passed out of a long intellectual pubescence. But many things preceded it.

First of all, the reason I did not set foot on a university campus for so long was the massive war protests I returned to. In spite of later convictions about that conflict and a growing liberal view insofar as the treatment of all people was concerned, I was not in agreement with the hedonism of the hippy movement, though I know now that they had simply made the existing hedonism more apparent.

I still find the hedonism distasteful, a kind of poison affecting many better convictions for the worst. Perhaps it is because, in the end, for most people the impulses of the body come first and thus quietly, even secretly, distort every other possibly good- or well-intended motive. To this day we have good ideas and bad impulses. It is the ongoing story of humanity. One step forward in ideas, two steps backward in impulses.

God (or the spirit, as I understand it) only knows if this will ever change. But I hope so. It took me a long time to see any light – what little I have seen. Before I went to graduate school I did meet my present wife, whom I have been happily married to for the last forty-three years. She also has an intellectual nature, though slightly different interests, and she went on to obtain a bachelors and two maters degrees during our marriage. She has written a number of very good, carefully researched historical novels about Mexican and American pre-statehood New Mexico.

Coincidentally, my first wife met someone and also remarried in the same year – in 1981. Her marriage lasted until the death of her husband. So it would seem we both had made a mistake and were able to correct it in later years. The tragedy is always the suffering this produces in the children. I deeply regret this.

I should probably briefly explain some of the mysteries of my psychological state after I came home from Vietnam. I had nightmares which I did not remember and was depressed for twelve years. Then I had a particularly poignant nightmare that ended it all. I dreamed I got into a hand-to-hand fight (no weapons) with a Viet Cong, and I drowned him in a rice paddy. This released something in me, and I remembered the other dreams, which had been repeated over those years. No such dreams ever occurred after that. It was over.

The dreams were never dramatic combat events. They were always of such things as my fellow Marines hanging from gibbets, bodies being tossed from a truck in body bags and bursting on the road, bodies hidden in a basement, for which I was somehow responsible, though I did not know how. Always the dreams were about wasteful death and were nauseating, and there was a helpless sense of personal responsibility for their content. It was good when they ended, and the depression passed away with them. Within a year of this, I met my second wife, and we were married. We have two sons.

www.ingramcontent.com/pod-product-compliance
Lightning Source LLC
Chambersburg PA
CBHW070056080526
44586CB00013B/1088